The Life and Death of Richard The Third

A Play By
William Shakespeare

The Life and Death of Richard The Third

by William Shakespeare

Copyright © 2022

All Rights reserved.
No part of this publication may be reproduced, stored in a retrieval system, or transmitted in any form or by any means, electronic, mechanical, photocopying or Otherwise, without the written permission of the publisher.

The author/editor asserts the moral right to be identified as the author/editor of this work.

ISBN: 978-93-94973-63-3

Published by

DOUBLE 9 BOOKS

2/13-B, Ansari Road
Daryaganj, New Delhi - 110002
info@double9books.com
www.double9books.com
Tel. 011-40042856

This book is under public domain

Printed in India.

About the Author

William Shakespeare was an English artist and dramatist, broadly viewed as the best essayist in the English language and one of the world's pre-famous playwrights. His magnetic works comprise 38 plays, 154 pieces, two long story sonnets, and a few other sonnets.

Shakespeare was brought up in Stratford-upon-Avon. He was 18 when he got married to Anne Hathaway, with whom he had three kids: Susanna, and twins Hamnet and Judith. Somewhere in the period between 1585 and 1592, he started to professionally work in London as an entertainer, author, and part proprietor of the playing organization then called 'the Lord Chamberlain's Men', later known as the King's Men'. Very few records on Shakespeare's personal life have been collected by now which has led to significant speculations and research on matters such as his sexuality, strict convictions, and whether the works ascribed to him were composed by others.

Shakespeare delivered the greater part of his known work somewhere between 1590 and 1613. He was a highly regarded writer and dramatist in his days. However, his standing didn't ascend to its current statures until the nineteenth century. The Romantics acclaimed Shakespeare as a virtuoso and the legends of the Victorian era adored him. Irish novelist, Bernard Shaw termed the word 'bardolatry' in his honor. In the 20th century, his work was rediscovered by new developments in grant and execution.

Contents

ACT I
- SCENE I. London. A street. ... 7
- SCENE II. The same. Another street. ... 13
- SCENE III. The palace. ... 24
- SCENE IV. London. The Tower. ... 38

ACT II
- SCENE I. London. The palace. ... 50
- SCENE II. The palace. ... 55
- SCENE III. London. A street. ... 61
- SCENE IV. London. The palace. ... 64

ACT III
- SCENE I. London. A street. ... 68
- SCENE II. Before Lord Hastings' house. ... 77
- SCENE III. Pomfret Castle. ... 82
- SCENE IV. The Tower of London. ... 83
- SCENE V. The Tower-walls. ... 88
- SCENE VI. The same. ... 92
- SCENE VII. Baynard's Castle. ... 92

ACT IV
- SCENE I. Before the Tower. ... 102
- SCENE II. London. The palace. ... 106
- SCENE III. The same. ... 112
- SCENE IV. Before the palace. ... 115
- SCENE V. Lord Derby's house. ... 137

ACT V
- SCENE I. Salisbury. An open place. ... 138
- SCENE II. The camp near Tamworth. ... 139
- SCENE III. Bosworth Field. ... 140
- SCENE IV. Another part of the field. ... 156
- SCENE V. Another part of the field. ... 157

ACT I

SCENE I. London.
A street.

Enter GLOUCESTER, solus

GLOUCESTER
Now is the winter of our discontent
Made glorious summer by this sun of York;
And all the clouds that lour'd upon our house
In the deep bosom of the ocean buried.
Now are our brows bound with victorious wreaths;
Our bruised arms hung up for monuments;

Our stern alarums changed to merry meetings,
Our dreadful marches to delightful measures.
Grim-visaged war hath smooth'd his wrinkled front;
And now, instead of mounting barded steeds
To fright the souls of fearful adversaries,
He capers nimbly in a lady's chamber
To the lascivious pleasing of a lute.
But I, that am not shaped for sportive tricks,
Nor made to court an amorous looking-glass;
I, that am rudely stamp'd, and want love's majesty
To strut before a wanton ambling nymph;
I, that am curtail'd of this fair proportion,
Cheated of feature by dissembling nature,
Deformed, unfinish'd, sent before my time
Into this breathing world, scarce half made up,
And that so lamely and unfashionable

That dogs bark at me as I halt by them;
Why, I, in this weak piping time of peace,
Have no delight to pass away the time,
Unless to spy my shadow in the sun
And descant on mine own deformity:
And therefore, since I cannot prove a lover,
To entertain these fair well-spoken days,
I am determined to prove a villain
And hate the idle pleasures of these days.
Plots have I laid, inductions dangerous,
By drunken prophecies, libels and dreams,
To set my brother Clarence and the king
In deadly hate the one against the other:
And if King Edward be as true and just
As I am subtle, false and treacherous,
This day should Clarence closely be mew'd up,
About a prophecy, which says that 'G'
Of Edward's heirs the murderer shall be.
Dive, thoughts, down to my soul: here
Clarence comes.

Enter CLARENCE, guarded, and BRAKENBURY

Brother, good day; what means this armed guard
That waits upon your grace?

CLARENCE

His majesty
Tendering my person's safety, hath appointed
This conduct to convey me to the Tower.

GLOUCESTER

Upon what cause?

CLARENCE

Because my name is George.

GLOUCESTER

Alack, my lord, that fault is none of yours;
He should, for that, commit your godfathers:
O, belike his majesty hath some intent

That you shall be new-christen'd in the Tower.
But what's the matter, Clarence? may I know?

CLARENCE

Yea, Richard, when I know; for I protest
As yet I do not: but, as I can learn,
He hearkens after prophecies and dreams;
And from the cross-row plucks the letter G.
And says a wizard told him that by G
His issue disinherited should be;
And, for my name of George begins with G,
It follows in his thought that I am he.
These, as I learn, and such like toys as these
Have moved his highness to commit me now.

GLOUCESTER

Why, this it is, when men are ruled by women:
'Tis not the king that sends you to the Tower:
My Lady Grey his wife, Clarence, 'tis she
That tempers him to this extremity.
Was it not she and that good man of worship,
Anthony Woodville, her brother there,
That made him send Lord Hastings to the Tower,
From whence this present day he is deliver'd?
We are not safe, Clarence; we are not safe.

CLARENCE

By heaven, I think there's no man is secure
But the queen's kindred and night-walking heralds
That trudge betwixt the king and Mistress Shore.
Heard ye not what an humble suppliant
Lord hastings was to her for his delivery?

GLOUCESTER

Humbly complaining to her deity
Got my lord chamberlain his liberty.
I'll tell you what; I think it is our way,
If we will keep in favour with the king,
To be her men and wear her livery:
The jealous o'erworn widow and herself,

Since that our brother dubb'd them gentlewomen.
Are mighty gossips in this monarchy.

BRAKENBURY

I beseech your graces both to pardon me;
His majesty hath straitly given in charge
That no man shall have private conference,
Of what degree soever, with his brother.

GLOUCESTER

Even so; an't please your worship, Brakenbury,
You may partake of any thing we say:
We speak no treason, man: we say the king
Is wise and virtuous, and his noble queen
Well struck in years, fair, and not jealous;
We say that Shore's wife hath a pretty foot,
A cherry lip, a bonny eye, a passing pleasing tongue;
And that the queen's kindred are made gentle-folks:
How say you sir? Can you deny all this?

BRAKENBURY

With this, my lord, myself have nought to do.

GLOUCESTER

Naught to do with mistress Shore! I tell thee, fellow,
He that doth naught with her, excepting one,
Were best he do it secretly, alone.

BRAKENBURY

What one, my lord?

GLOUCESTER

Her husband, knave: wouldst thou betray me?

BRAKENBURY

I beseech your grace to pardon me, and withal
Forbear your conference with the noble duke.

CLARENCE

We know thy charge, Brakenbury, and will obey.

GLOUCESTER

We are the queen's abjects, and must obey.
Brother, farewell: I will unto the king;

And whatsoever you will employ me in,
Were it to call King Edward's widow sister,
I will perform it to enfranchise you.
Meantime, this deep disgrace in brotherhood
Touches me deeper than you can imagine.

CLARENCE

I know it pleaseth neither of us well.

GLOUCESTER

Well, your imprisonment shall not be long;
Meantime, have patience.

CLARENCE

I must perforce. Farewell.

Exeunt CLARENCE, BRAKENBURY, and Guard

GLOUCESTER

Go, tread the path that thou shalt ne'er return.
Simple, plain Clarence! I do love thee so,
That I will shortly send thy soul to heaven,
If heaven will take the present at our hands.
But who comes here? the new-deliver'd Hastings?

Enter HASTINGS

HASTINGS

Good time of day unto my gracious lord!

GLOUCESTER

As much unto my good lord chamberlain!
Well are you welcome to the open air.
How hath your lordship brook'd imprisonment?

HASTINGS

With patience, noble lord, as prisoners must:
But I shall live, my lord, to give them thanks
That were the cause of my imprisonment.

GLOUCESTER

No doubt, no doubt; and so shall Clarence too;
For they that were your enemies are his,
And have prevail'd as much on him as you.

HASTINGS

More pity that the eagle should be mew'd,
While kites and buzzards prey at liberty.

GLOUCESTER

What news abroad?

HASTINGS

No news so bad abroad as this at home;
The King is sickly, weak and melancholy,
And his physicians fear him mightily.

GLOUCESTER

Now, by Saint Paul, this news is bad indeed.
O, he hath kept an evil diet long,
And overmuch consumed his royal person:
'Tis very grievous to be thought upon.
What, is he in his bed?

HASTINGS

He is.

GLOUCESTER

Go you before, and I will follow you.

Exit HASTINGS

He cannot live, I hope; and must not die
Till George be pack'd with post-horse up to heaven.
I'll in, to urge his hatred more to Clarence,
With lies well steel'd with weighty arguments;
And, if I fall not in my deep intent,
Clarence hath not another day to live:
Which done, God take King Edward to his mercy,
And leave the world for me to bustle in!
For then I'll marry Warwick's youngest daughter.
What though I kill'd her husband and her father?
The readiest way to make the wench amends
Is to become her husband and her father:
The which will I; not all so much for love
As for another secret close intent,
By marrying her which I must reach unto.

But yet I run before my horse to market:
Clarence still breathes; Edward still lives and reigns:
When they are gone, then must I count my gains.

Exit

SCENE II. The same. Another street.

Enter the corpse of KING HENRY the Sixth, Gentlemen with halberds to guard it; LADY ANNE being the mourner

LADY ANNE
Set down, set down your honourable load,
If honour may be shrouded in a hearse,
Whilst I awhile obsequiously lament
The untimely fall of virtuous Lancaster.
Poor key-cold figure of a holy king!
Pale ashes of the house of Lancaster!
Thou bloodless remnant of that royal blood!
Be it lawful that I invocate thy ghost,
To hear the lamentations of Poor Anne,
Wife to thy Edward, to thy slaughter'd son,
Stabb'd by the selfsame hand that made these wounds!
Lo, in these windows that let forth thy life,
I pour the helpless balm of my poor eyes.
Cursed be the hand that made these fatal holes!
Cursed be the heart that had the heart to do it!
Cursed the blood that let this blood from hence!
More direful hap betide that hated wretch,
That makes us wretched by the death of thee,
Than I can wish to adders, spiders, toads,
Or any creeping venom'd thing that lives!
If ever he have child, abortive be it,
Prodigious, and untimely brought to light,
Whose ugly and unnatural aspect
May fright the hopeful mother at the view;
And that be heir to his unhappiness!
If ever he have wife, let her he made
A miserable by the death of him
As I am made by my poor lord and thee!
Come, now towards Chertsey with your holy load,

Taken from Paul's to be interred there;
And still, as you are weary of the weight,
Rest you, whiles I lament King Henry's corse.

Enter GLOUCESTER

GLOUCESTER

Stay, you that bear the corse, and set it down.

LADY ANNE

What black magician conjures up this fiend,
To stop devoted charitable deeds?

GLOUCESTER

Villains, set down the corse; or, by Saint Paul,
I'll make a corse of him that disobeys.

Gentleman

My lord, stand back, and let the coffin pass.

GLOUCESTER

Unmanner'd dog! stand thou, when I command:
Advance thy halbert higher than my breast,
Or, by Saint Paul, I'll strike thee to my foot,
And spurn upon thee, beggar, for thy boldness.

LADY ANNE

What, do you tremble? are you all afraid?
Alas, I blame you not; for you are mortal,
And mortal eyes cannot endure the devil.
Avaunt, thou dreadful minister of hell!
Thou hadst but power over his mortal body,
His soul thou canst not have; therefore be gone.

GLOUCESTER

Sweet saint, for charity, be not so curst.

LADY ANNE

Foul devil, for God's sake, hence, and trouble us not;
For thou hast made the happy earth thy hell,
Fill'd it with cursing cries and deep exclaims.
If thou delight to view thy heinous deeds,
Behold this pattern of thy butcheries.

O, gentlemen, see, see! dead Henry's wounds
Open their congeal'd mouths and bleed afresh!
Blush, Blush, thou lump of foul deformity;
For 'tis thy presence that exhales this blood
From cold and empty veins, where no blood dwells;
Thy deed, inhuman and unnatural,
Provokes this deluge most unnatural.
O God, which this blood madest, revenge his death!
O earth, which this blood drink'st revenge his death!
Either heaven with lightning strike the
murderer dead,
Or earth, gape open wide and eat him quick,
As thou dost swallow up this good king's blood
Which his hell-govern'd arm hath butchered!

GLOUCESTER

Lady, you know no rules of charity,
Which renders good for bad, blessings for curses.

LADY ANNE

Villain, thou know'st no law of God nor man:
No beast so fierce but knows some touch of pity.

GLOUCESTER

But I know none, and therefore am no beast.

LADY ANNE

O wonderful, when devils tell the truth!

GLOUCESTER

More wonderful, when angels are so angry.
Vouchsafe, divine perfection of a woman,
Of these supposed-evils, to give me leave,
By circumstance, but to acquit myself.

LADY ANNE

Vouchsafe, defused infection of a man,
For these known evils, but to give me leave,
By circumstance, to curse thy cursed self.

GLOUCESTER

Fairer than tongue can name thee, let me have
Some patient leisure to excuse myself.

LADY ANNE

Fouler than heart can think thee, thou canst make
No excuse current, but to hang thyself.

GLOUCESTER

By such despair, I should accuse myself.

LADY ANNE

And, by despairing, shouldst thou stand excused;
For doing worthy vengeance on thyself,
Which didst unworthy slaughter upon others.

GLOUCESTER

Say that I slew them not?

LADY ANNE

Why, then they are not dead:
But dead they are, and devilish slave, by thee.

GLOUCESTER

I did not kill your husband.

LADY ANNE

Why, then he is alive.

GLOUCESTER

Nay, he is dead; and slain by Edward's hand.

LADY ANNE

In thy foul throat thou liest: Queen Margaret saw
Thy murderous falchion smoking in his blood;
The which thou once didst bend against her breast,
But that thy brothers beat aside the point.

GLOUCESTER

I was provoked by her slanderous tongue,
which laid their guilt upon my guiltless shoulders.

LADY ANNE

Thou wast provoked by thy bloody mind.
Which never dreamt on aught but butcheries:
Didst thou not kill this king?

GLOUCESTER

I grant ye.

LADY ANNE

Dost grant me, hedgehog? then, God grant me too
Thou mayst be damned for that wicked deed!
O, he was gentle, mild, and virtuous!

GLOUCESTER

The fitter for the King of heaven, that hath him.

LADY ANNE

He is in heaven, where thou shalt never come.

GLOUCESTER

Let him thank me, that holp to send him thither;
For he was fitter for that place than earth.

LADY ANNE

And thou unfit for any place but hell.

GLOUCESTER

Yes, one place else, if you will hear me name it.

LADY ANNE

Some dungeon.

GLOUCESTER

Your bed-chamber.

LADY ANNE

I'll rest betide the chamber where thou liest!

GLOUCESTER

So will it, madam till I lie with you.

LADY ANNE

I hope so.

GLOUCESTER

I know so. But, gentle Lady Anne,
To leave this keen encounter of our wits,
And fall somewhat into a slower method,
Is not the causer of the timeless deaths
Of these Plantagenets, Henry and Edward,
As blameful as the executioner?

LADY ANNE

Thou art the cause, and most accursed effect.

GLOUCESTER

Your beauty was the cause of that effect;
Your beauty: which did haunt me in my sleep
To undertake the death of all the world,
So I might live one hour in your sweet bosom.

LADY ANNE

If I thought that, I tell thee, homicide,
These nails should rend that beauty from my cheeks.

GLOUCESTER

These eyes could never endure sweet beauty's wreck;
You should not blemish it, if I stood by:
As all the world is cheered by the sun,
So I by that; it is my day, my life.

LADY ANNE

Black night o'ershade thy day, and death thy life!

GLOUCESTER

Curse not thyself, fair creature thou art both.

LADY ANNE

I would I were, to be revenged on thee.

GLOUCESTER

It is a quarrel most unnatural,
To be revenged on him that loveth you.

LADY ANNE

It is a quarrel just and reasonable,
To be revenged on him that slew my husband.

GLOUCESTER

He that bereft thee, lady, of thy husband,
Did it to help thee to a better husband.

LADY ANNE

His better doth not breathe upon the earth.

GLOUCESTER

He lives that loves thee better than he could.

LADY ANNE
Name him.

GLOUCESTER
Plantagenet.

LADY ANNE
Why, that was he.

GLOUCESTER
The selfsame name, but one of better nature.

LADY ANNE
Where is he?

GLOUCESTER
Here.
She spitteth at him
Why dost thou spit at me?

LADY ANNE
Would it were mortal poison, for thy sake!

GLOUCESTER
Never came poison from so sweet a place.

LADY ANNE
Never hung poison on a fouler toad.
Out of my sight! thou dost infect my eyes.

GLOUCESTER
Thine eyes, sweet lady, have infected mine.

LADY ANNE
Would they were basilisks, to strike thee dead!

GLOUCESTER
I would they were, that I might die at once;
For now they kill me with a living death.
Those eyes of thine from mine have drawn salt tears,
Shamed their aspect with store of childish drops:
These eyes that never shed remorseful tear,
No, when my father York and Edward wept,

To hear the piteous moan that Rutland made
When black-faced Clifford shook his sword at him;
Nor when thy warlike father, like a child,
Told the sad story of my father's death,
And twenty times made pause to sob and weep,
That all the standers-by had wet their cheeks
Like trees bedash'd with rain: in that sad time
My manly eyes did scorn an humble tear;
And what these sorrows could not thence exhale,
Thy beauty hath, and made them blind with weeping.
I never sued to friend nor enemy;
My tongue could never learn sweet smoothing word;
But now thy beauty is proposed my fee,
My proud heart sues, and prompts my tongue to speak.

She looks scornfully at him

Teach not thy lips such scorn, for they were made
For kissing, lady, not for such contempt.
If thy revengeful heart cannot forgive,
Lo, here I lend thee this sharp-pointed sword;
Which if thou please to hide in this true bosom.
And let the soul forth that adoreth thee,
I lay it naked to the deadly stroke,
And humbly beg the death upon my knee.

He lays his breast open: she offers at it with his sword

Nay, do not pause; for I did kill King Henry,
But 'twas thy beauty that provoked me.
Nay, now dispatch; 'twas I that stabb'd young Edward,
But 'twas thy heavenly face that set me on.

Here she lets fall the sword

Take up the sword again, or take up me.

LADY ANNE

Arise, dissembler: though I wish thy death,
I will not be the executioner.

GLOUCESTER

Then bid me kill myself, and I will do it.

LADY ANNE

I have already.

GLOUCESTER

Tush, that was in thy rage:
Speak it again, and, even with the word,
That hand, which, for thy love, did kill thy love,
Shall, for thy love, kill a far truer love;
To both their deaths thou shalt be accessary.

LADY ANNE

I would I knew thy heart.

GLOUCESTER

'Tis figured in my tongue.

LADY ANNE

I fear me both are false.

GLOUCESTER

Then never man was true.

LADY ANNE

Well, well, put up your sword.

GLOUCESTER

Say, then, my peace is made.

LADY ANNE

That shall you know hereafter.

GLOUCESTER

But shall I live in hope?

LADY ANNE

All men, I hope, live so.

GLOUCESTER

Vouchsafe to wear this ring.

LADY ANNE

To take is not to give.

GLOUCESTER

Look, how this ring encompasseth finger.
Even so thy breast encloseth my poor heart;

Wear both of them, for both of them are thine.
And if thy poor devoted suppliant may
But beg one favour at thy gracious hand,
Thou dost confirm his happiness for ever.

LADY ANNE

What is it?

GLOUCESTER

That it would please thee leave these sad designs
To him that hath more cause to be a mourner,
And presently repair to Crosby Place;
Where, after I have solemnly interr'd
At Chertsey monastery this noble king,
And wet his grave with my repentant tears,
I will with all expedient duty see you:
For divers unknown reasons. I beseech you,
Grant me this boon.

LADY ANNE

With all my heart; and much it joys me too,
To see you are become so penitent.
Tressel and Berkeley, go along with me.

GLOUCESTER

Bid me farewell.

LADY ANNE

'Tis more than you deserve;
But since you teach me how to flatter you,
Imagine I have said farewell already.

Exeunt LADY ANNE, TRESSEL, and BERKELEY

GLOUCESTER

Sirs, take up the corse.

GENTLEMEN

Towards Chertsey, noble lord?

GLOUCESTER

No, to White-Friars; there attend my coining.

Exeunt all but GLOUCESTER

Was ever woman in this humour woo'd?
Was ever woman in this humour won?
I'll have her; but I will not keep her long.
What! I, that kill'd her husband and his father,
To take her in her heart's extremest hate,
With curses in her mouth, tears in her eyes,
The bleeding witness of her hatred by;
Having God, her conscience, and these bars against me,
And I nothing to back my suit at all,
But the plain devil and dissembling looks,
And yet to win her, all the world to nothing!
Ha!
Hath she forgot already that brave prince,
Edward, her lord, whom I, some three months since,
Stabb'd in my angry mood at Tewksbury?
A sweeter and a lovelier gentleman,
Framed in the prodigality of nature,
Young, valiant, wise, and, no doubt, right royal,
The spacious world cannot again afford
And will she yet debase her eyes on me,
That cropp'd the golden prime of this sweet prince,
And made her widow to a woful bed?
On me, whose all not equals Edward's moiety?
On me, that halt and am unshapen thus?
My dukedom to a beggarly denier,
I do mistake my person all this while:
Upon my life, she finds, although I cannot,
Myself to be a marvellous proper man.
I'll be at charges for a looking-glass,
And entertain some score or two of tailors,
To study fashions to adorn my body:
Since I am crept in favour with myself,
Will maintain it with some little cost.
But first I'll turn yon fellow in his grave;
And then return lamenting to my love.
Shine out, fair sun, till I have bought a glass,
That I may see my shadow as I pass.

Exit

SCENE III. The palace.

Enter QUEEN ELIZABETH, RIVERS, and GREY

RIVERS

Have patience, madam: there's no doubt his majesty
Will soon recover his accustom'd health.

GREY

In that you brook it in, it makes him worse:
Therefore, for God's sake, entertain good comfort,
And cheer his grace with quick and merry words.

QUEEN ELIZABETH

If he were dead, what would betide of me?

RIVERS

No other harm but loss of such a lord.

QUEEN ELIZABETH

The loss of such a lord includes all harm.

GREY

The heavens have bless'd you with a goodly son,
To be your comforter when he is gone.

QUEEN ELIZABETH

Oh, he is young and his minority
Is put unto the trust of Richard Gloucester,
A man that loves not me, nor none of you.

RIVERS

Is it concluded that he shall be protector?

QUEEN ELIZABETH

It is determined, not concluded yet:
But so it must be, if the king miscarry.

Enter BUCKINGHAM and DERBY

GREY

Here come the lords of Buckingham and Derby.

BUCKINGHAM

Good time of day unto your royal grace!

DERBY

God make your majesty joyful as you have been!

QUEEN ELIZABETH

The Countess Richmond, good my Lord of Derby.
To your good prayers will scarcely say amen.
Yet, Derby, notwithstanding she's your wife,
And loves not me, be you, good lord, assured
I hate not you for her proud arrogance.

DERBY

I do beseech you, either not believe
The envious slanders of her false accusers;
Or, if she be accused in true report,
Bear with her weakness, which, I think proceeds
From wayward sickness, and no grounded malice.

RIVERS

Saw you the king to-day, my Lord of Derby?

DERBY

But now the Duke of Buckingham and I
Are come from visiting his majesty.

QUEEN ELIZABETH

What likelihood of his amendment, lords?

BUCKINGHAM

Madam, good hope; his grace speaks cheerfully.

QUEEN ELIZABETH

God grant him health! Did you confer with him?

BUCKINGHAM

Madam, we did: he desires to make atonement
Betwixt the Duke of Gloucester and your brothers,
And betwixt them and my lord chamberlain;
And sent to warn them to his royal presence.

QUEEN ELIZABETH

Would all were well! but that will never be
I fear our happiness is at the highest.

Enter GLOUCESTER, HASTINGS, and DORSET

GLOUCESTER

They do me wrong, and I will not endure it:
Who are they that complain unto the king,
That I, forsooth, am stern, and love them not?
By holy Paul, they love his grace but lightly
That fill his ears with such dissentious rumours.
Because I cannot flatter and speak fair,
Smile in men's faces, smooth, deceive and cog,
Duck with French nods and apish courtesy,
I must be held a rancorous enemy.
Cannot a plain man live and think no harm,
But thus his simple truth must be abused
By silken, sly, insinuating Jacks?

RIVERS

To whom in all this presence speaks your grace?

GLOUCESTER

To thee, that hast nor honesty nor grace.
When have I injured thee? when done thee wrong?
Or thee? or thee? or any of your faction?
A plague upon you all! His royal person,--
Whom God preserve better than you would wish!--
Cannot be quiet scarce a breathing-while,
But you must trouble him with lewd complaints.

QUEEN ELIZABETH

Brother of Gloucester, you mistake the matter.
The king, of his own royal disposition,
And not provoked by any suitor else;
Aiming, belike, at your interior hatred,
Which in your outward actions shows itself
Against my kindred, brothers, and myself,
Makes him to send; that thereby he may gather
The ground of your ill-will, and so remove it.

GLOUCESTER

I cannot tell: the world is grown so bad,
That wrens make prey where eagles dare not perch:

Since every Jack became a gentleman
There's many a gentle person made a Jack.

QUEEN ELIZABETH

Come, come, we know your meaning, brother Gloucester;
You envy my advancement and my friends':
God grant we never may have need of you!

GLOUCESTER

Meantime, God grants that we have need of you:
Your brother is imprison'd by your means,
Myself disgraced, and the nobility
Held in contempt; whilst many fair promotions
Are daily given to ennoble those
That scarce, some two days since, were worth a noble.

QUEEN ELIZABETH

By Him that raised me to this careful height
From that contented hap which I enjoy'd,
I never did incense his majesty
Against the Duke of Clarence, but have been
An earnest advocate to plead for him.
My lord, you do me shameful injury,
Falsely to draw me in these vile suspects.

GLOUCESTER

You may deny that you were not the cause
Of my Lord Hastings' late imprisonment.

RIVERS

She may, my lord, for--

GLOUCESTER

She may, Lord Rivers! why, who knows not so?
She may do more, sir, than denying that:
She may help you to many fair preferments,
And then deny her aiding hand therein,
And lay those honours on your high deserts.
What may she not? She may, yea, marry, may she--

RIVERS

What, marry, may she?

GLOUCESTER

What, marry, may she! marry with a king,
A bachelor, a handsome stripling too:
I wis your grandam had a worser match.

QUEEN ELIZABETH

My Lord of Gloucester, I have too long borne
Your blunt upbraidings and your bitter scoffs:
By heaven, I will acquaint his majesty
With those gross taunts I often have endured.
I had rather be a country servant-maid
Than a great queen, with this condition,
To be thus taunted, scorn'd, and baited at:

Enter QUEEN MARGARET, behind

Small joy have I in being England's queen.

QUEEN MARGARET

And lessen'd be that small, God, I beseech thee!
Thy honour, state and seat is due to me.

GLOUCESTER

What! threat you me with telling of the king?
Tell him, and spare not: look, what I have said
I will avouch in presence of the king:
I dare adventure to be sent to the Tower.
'Tis time to speak; my pains are quite forgot.

QUEEN MARGARET

Out, devil! I remember them too well:
Thou slewest my husband Henry in the Tower,
And Edward, my poor son, at Tewksbury.

GLOUCESTER

Ere you were queen, yea, or your husband king,
I was a pack-horse in his great affairs;
A weeder-out of his proud adversaries,
A liberal rewarder of his friends:
To royalize his blood I spilt mine own.

QUEEN MARGARET

Yea, and much better blood than his or thine.

GLOUCESTER

In all which time you and your husband Grey
Were factious for the house of Lancaster;
And, Rivers, so were you. Was not your husband
In Margaret's battle at Saint Alban's slain?
Let me put in your minds, if you forget,
What you have been ere now, and what you are;
Withal, what I have been, and what I am.

QUEEN MARGARET

A murderous villain, and so still thou art.

GLOUCESTER

Poor Clarence did forsake his father, Warwick;
Yea, and forswore himself,--which Jesu pardon!--

QUEEN MARGARET

Which God revenge!

GLOUCESTER

To fight on Edward's party for the crown;
And for his meed, poor lord, he is mew'd up.
I would to God my heart were flint, like Edward's;
Or Edward's soft and pitiful, like mine
I am too childish-foolish for this world.

QUEEN MARGARET

Hie thee to hell for shame, and leave the world,
Thou cacodemon! there thy kingdom is.

RIVERS

My Lord of Gloucester, in those busy days
Which here you urge to prove us enemies,
We follow'd then our lord, our lawful king:
So should we you, if you should be our king.

GLOUCESTER

If I should be! I had rather be a pedlar:
Far be it from my heart, the thought of it!

QUEEN ELIZABETH

As little joy, my lord, as you suppose
You should enjoy, were you this country's king,
As little joy may you suppose in me.
That I enjoy, being the queen thereof.

QUEEN MARGARET

A little joy enjoys the queen thereof;
For I am she, and altogether joyless.
I can no longer hold me patient.

Advancing

Hear me, you wrangling pirates, that fall out
In sharing that which you have pill'd from me!
Which of you trembles not that looks on me?
If not, that, I being queen, you bow like subjects,
Yet that, by you deposed, you quake like rebels?
O gentle villain, do not turn away!

GLOUCESTER

Foul wrinkled witch, what makest thou in my sight?

QUEEN MARGARET

But repetition of what thou hast marr'd;
That will I make before I let thee go.

GLOUCESTER

Wert thou not banished on pain of death?

QUEEN MARGARET

I was; but I do find more pain in banishment
Than death can yield me here by my abode.
A husband and a son thou owest to me;
And thou a kingdom; all of you allegiance:
The sorrow that I have, by right is yours,
And all the pleasures you usurp are mine.

GLOUCESTER

The curse my noble father laid on thee,
When thou didst crown his warlike brows with paper
And with thy scorns drew'st rivers from his eyes,
And then, to dry them, gavest the duke a clout

Steep'd in the faultless blood of pretty Rutland--
His curses, then from bitterness of soul
Denounced against thee, are all fall'n upon thee;
And God, not we, hath plagued thy bloody deed.

QUEEN ELIZABETH

So just is God, to right the innocent.

HASTINGS

O, 'twas the foulest deed to slay that babe,
And the most merciless that e'er was heard of!

RIVERS

Tyrants themselves wept when it was reported.

DORSET

No man but prophesied revenge for it.

BUCKINGHAM

Northumberland, then present, wept to see it.

QUEEN MARGARET

What were you snarling all before I came,
Ready to catch each other by the throat,
And turn you all your hatred now on me?
Did York's dread curse prevail so much with heaven?
That Henry's death, my lovely Edward's death,
Their kingdom's loss, my woful banishment,
Could all but answer for that peevish brat?
Can curses pierce the clouds and enter heaven?
Why, then, give way, dull clouds, to my quick curses!
If not by war, by surfeit die your king,
As ours by murder, to make him a king!
Edward thy son, which now is Prince of Wales,
For Edward my son, which was Prince of Wales,
Die in his youth by like untimely violence!
Thyself a queen, for me that was a queen,
Outlive thy glory, like my wretched self!
Long mayst thou live to wail thy children's loss;
And see another, as I see thee now,

Deck'd in thy rights, as thou art stall'd in mine!
Long die thy happy days before thy death;
And, after many lengthen'd hours of grief,
Die neither mother, wife, nor England's queen!
Rivers and Dorset, you were standers by,
And so wast thou, Lord Hastings, when my son
Was stabb'd with bloody daggers: God, I pray him,
That none of you may live your natural age,
But by some unlook'd accident cut off!

GLOUCESTER

Have done thy charm, thou hateful wither'd hag!

QUEEN MARGARET

And leave out thee? stay, dog, for thou shalt hear me.
If heaven have any grievous plague in store
Exceeding those that I can wish upon thee,
O, let them keep it till thy sins be ripe,
And then hurl down their indignation
On thee, the troubler of the poor world's peace!
The worm of conscience still begnaw thy soul!
Thy friends suspect for traitors while thou livest,
And take deep traitors for thy dearest friends!
No sleep close up that deadly eye of thine,
Unless it be whilst some tormenting dream
Affrights thee with a hell of ugly devils!
Thou elvish-mark'd, abortive, rooting hog!
Thou that wast seal'd in thy nativity
The slave of nature and the son of hell!
Thou slander of thy mother's heavy womb!
Thou loathed issue of thy father's loins!
Thou rag of honour! thou detested--

GLOUCESTER

Margaret.

QUEEN MARGARET

Richard!

GLOUCESTER

Ha!

QUEEN MARGARET

I call thee not.

GLOUCESTER

I cry thee mercy then, for I had thought
That thou hadst call'd me all these bitter names.

QUEEN MARGARET

Why, so I did; but look'd for no reply.
O, let me make the period to my curse!

GLOUCESTER

'Tis done by me, and ends in 'Margaret.'

QUEEN ELIZABETH

Thus have you breathed your curse against yourself.

QUEEN MARGARET

Poor painted queen, vain flourish of my fortune!
Why strew'st thou sugar on that bottled spider,
Whose deadly web ensnareth thee about?
Fool, fool! thou whet'st a knife to kill thyself.
The time will come when thou shalt wish for me
To help thee curse that poisonous bunchback'd toad.

HASTINGS

False-boding woman, end thy frantic curse,
Lest to thy harm thou move our patience.

QUEEN MARGARET

Foul shame upon you! you have all moved mine.

RIVERS

Were you well served, you would be taught your duty.

QUEEN MARGARET

To serve me well, you all should do me duty,
Teach me to be your queen, and you my subjects:
O, serve me well, and teach yourselves that duty!

DORSET

Dispute not with her; she is lunatic.

QUEEN MARGARET

Peace, master marquess, you are malapert:
Your fire-new stamp of honour is scarce current.
O, that your young nobility could judge
What 'twere to lose it, and be miserable!
They that stand high have many blasts to shake them;
And if they fall, they dash themselves to pieces.

GLOUCESTER

Good counsel, marry: learn it, learn it, marquess.

DORSET

It toucheth you, my lord, as much as me.

GLOUCESTER

Yea, and much more: but I was born so high,
Our aery buildeth in the cedar's top,
And dallies with the wind and scorns the sun.

QUEEN MARGARET

And turns the sun to shade; alas! alas!
Witness my son, now in the shade of death;
Whose bright out-shining beams thy cloudy wrath
Hath in eternal darkness folded up.
Your aery buildeth in our aery's nest.
O God, that seest it, do not suffer it!
As it was won with blood, lost be it so!

BUCKINGHAM

Have done! for shame, if not for charity.

QUEEN MARGARET

Urge neither charity nor shame to me:
Uncharitably with me have you dealt,
And shamefully by you my hopes are butcher'd.
My charity is outrage, life my shame
And in that shame still live my sorrow's rage.

BUCKINGHAM

Have done, have done.

QUEEN MARGARET

O princely Buckingham I'll kiss thy hand,
In sign of league and amity with thee:
Now fair befal thee and thy noble house!
Thy garments are not spotted with our blood,
Nor thou within the compass of my curse.

BUCKINGHAM

Nor no one here; for curses never pass
The lips of those that breathe them in the air.

QUEEN MARGARET

I'll not believe but they ascend the sky,
And there awake God's gentle-sleeping peace.
O Buckingham, take heed of yonder dog!
Look, when he fawns, he bites; and when he bites,
His venom tooth will rankle to the death:
Have not to do with him, beware of him;
Sin, death, and hell have set their marks on him,
And all their ministers attend on him.

GLOUCESTER

What doth she say, my Lord of Buckingham?

BUCKINGHAM

Nothing that I respect, my gracious lord.

QUEEN MARGARET

What, dost thou scorn me for my gentle counsel?
And soothe the devil that I warn thee from?
O, but remember this another day,
When he shall split thy very heart with sorrow,
And say poor Margaret was a prophetess!
Live each of you the subjects to his hate,
And he to yours, and all of you to God's!

Exit

HASTINGS

My hair doth stand on end to hear her curses.

RIVERS

And so doth mine: I muse why she's at liberty.

GLOUCESTER

I cannot blame her: by God's holy mother,
She hath had too much wrong; and I repent
My part thereof that I have done to her.

QUEEN ELIZABETH

I never did her any, to my knowledge.

GLOUCESTER

But you have all the vantage of her wrong.
I was too hot to do somebody good,
That is too cold in thinking of it now.
Marry, as for Clarence, he is well repaid,
He is frank'd up to fatting for his pains
God pardon them that are the cause of it!

RIVERS

A virtuous and a Christian-like conclusion,
To pray for them that have done scathe to us.

GLOUCESTER

So do I ever:

Aside

being well-advised.
For had I cursed now, I had cursed myself.

Enter CATESBY

CATESBY

Madam, his majesty doth call for you,
And for your grace; and you, my noble lords.

QUEEN ELIZABETH

Catesby, we come. Lords, will you go with us?

RIVERS

Madam, we will attend your grace.

Exeunt all but GLOUCESTER

GLOUCESTER

I do the wrong, and first begin to brawl.
The secret mischiefs that I set abroach
I lay unto the grievous charge of others.
Clarence, whom I, indeed, have laid in darkness,
I do beweep to many simple gulls
Namely, to Hastings, Derby, Buckingham;
And say it is the queen and her allies
That stir the king against the duke my brother.
Now, they believe it; and withal whet me
To be revenged on Rivers, Vaughan, Grey:
But then I sigh; and, with a piece of scripture,
Tell them that God bids us do good for evil:
And thus I clothe my naked villany
With old odd ends stolen out of holy writ;
And seem a saint, when most I play the devil.

Enter two Murderers

But, soft! here come my executioners.
How now, my hardy, stout resolved mates!
Are you now going to dispatch this deed?

First Murderer

We are, my lord; and come to have the warrant
That we may be admitted where he is.

GLOUCESTER

Well thought upon; I have it here about me.

Gives the warrant

When you have done, repair to Crosby Place.
But, sirs, be sudden in the execution,
Withal obdurate, do not hear him plead;
For Clarence is well-spoken, and perhaps
May move your hearts to pity if you mark him.

First Murderer

Tush!
Fear not, my lord, we will not stand to prate;

Talkers are no good doers: be assured
We come to use our hands and not our tongues.

GLOUCESTER

Your eyes drop millstones, when fools' eyes drop tears:
I like you, lads; about your business straight;
Go, go, dispatch.

First Murderer

We will, my noble lord.

Exeunt

SCENE IV. London. The Tower.

Enter CLARENCE and BRAKENBURY

BRAKENBURY

Why looks your grace so heavily today?

CLARENCE

O, I have pass'd a miserable night,
So full of ugly sights, of ghastly dreams,
That, as I am a Christian faithful man,
I would not spend another such a night,
Though 'twere to buy a world of happy days,
So full of dismal terror was the time!

BRAKENBURY

What was your dream? I long to hear you tell it.

CLARENCE

Methoughts that I had broken from the Tower,
And was embark'd to cross to Burgundy;
And, in my company, my brother Gloucester;
Who from my cabin tempted me to walk
Upon the hatches: thence we looked toward England,
And cited up a thousand fearful times,
During the wars of York and Lancaster
That had befall'n us. As we paced along
Upon the giddy footing of the hatches,
Methought that Gloucester stumbled; and, in falling,
Struck me, that thought to stay him, overboard,

Into the tumbling billows of the main.
Lord, Lord! methought, what pain it was to drown!
What dreadful noise of waters in mine ears!
What ugly sights of death within mine eyes!
Methought I saw a thousand fearful wrecks;
Ten thousand men that fishes gnaw'd upon;
Wedges of gold, great anchors, heaps of pearl,
Inestimable stones, unvalued jewels,
All scatter'd in the bottom of the sea:
Some lay in dead men's skulls; and, in those holes
Where eyes did once inhabit, there were crept,
As 'twere in scorn of eyes, reflecting gems,
Which woo'd the slimy bottom of the deep,
And mock'd the dead bones that lay scatter'd by.

BRAKENBURY

Had you such leisure in the time of death
To gaze upon the secrets of the deep?

CLARENCE

Methought I had; and often did I strive
To yield the ghost: but still the envious flood
Kept in my soul, and would not let it forth
To seek the empty, vast and wandering air;
But smother'd it within my panting bulk,
Which almost burst to belch it in the sea.

BRAKENBURY

Awaked you not with this sore agony?

CLARENCE

O, no, my dream was lengthen'd after life;
O, then began the tempest to my soul,
Who pass'd, methought, the melancholy flood,
With that grim ferryman which poets write of,
Unto the kingdom of perpetual night.
The first that there did greet my stranger soul,
Was my great father-in-law, renowned Warwick;
Who cried aloud, 'What scourge for perjury
Can this dark monarchy afford false Clarence?'
And so he vanish'd: then came wandering by

A shadow like an angel, with bright hair
Dabbled in blood; and he squeak'd out aloud,
'Clarence is come; false, fleeting, perjured Clarence,
That stabb'd me in the field by Tewksbury;
Seize on him, Furies, take him to your torments!'
With that, methoughts, a legion of foul fiends
Environ'd me about, and howled in mine ears
Such hideous cries, that with the very noise
I trembling waked, and for a season after
Could not believe but that I was in hell,
Such terrible impression made the dream.

BRAKENBURY

No marvel, my lord, though it affrighted you;
I promise, I am afraid to hear you tell it.

CLARENCE

O Brakenbury, I have done those things,
Which now bear evidence against my soul,
For Edward's sake; and see how he requites me!
O God! if my deep prayers cannot appease thee,
But thou wilt be avenged on my misdeeds,
Yet execute thy wrath in me alone,
O, spare my guiltless wife and my poor children!
I pray thee, gentle keeper, stay by me;
My soul is heavy, and I fain would sleep.

BRAKENBURY

I will, my lord: God give your grace good rest!

CLARENCE sleeps

Sorrow breaks seasons and reposing hours,
Makes the night morning, and the noon-tide night.
Princes have but their tides for their glories,
An outward honour for an inward toil;
And, for unfelt imagination,
They often feel a world of restless cares:
So that, betwixt their tides and low names,
There's nothing differs but the outward fame.

Enter the two Murderers

First Murderer

Ho! who's here?

BRAKENBURY

In God's name what are you, and how came you hither?

First Murderer

I would speak with Clarence, and I came hither on my legs.

BRAKENBURY

Yea, are you so brief?

Second Murderer

O sir, it is better to be brief than tedious. Show him our commission; talk no more.

BRAKENBURY reads it

BRAKENBURY

I am, in this, commanded to deliver
The noble Duke of Clarence to your hands:
I will not reason what is meant hereby,
Because I will be guiltless of the meaning.
Here are the keys, there sits the duke asleep:
I'll to the king; and signify to him
That thus I have resign'd my charge to you.

First Murderer

Do so, it is a point of wisdom: fare you well.

Exit BRAKENBURY

Second Murderer

What, shall we stab him as he sleeps?

First Murderer

No; then he will say 'twas done cowardly, when he wakes.

Second Murderer

When he wakes! why, fool, he shall never wake till the judgment-day.

First Murderer

Why, then he will say we stabbed him sleeping.

Second Murderer

The urging of that word 'judgment' hath bred a kind of remorse in me.

First Murderer

What, art thou afraid?

Second Murderer

Not to kill him, having a warrant for it; but to be damned for killing him, from which no warrant can defend us.

First Murderer

I thought thou hadst been resolute.

Second Murderer

So I am, to let him live.

First Murderer

Back to the Duke of Gloucester, tell him so.

Second Murderer

I pray thee, stay a while: I hope my holy humour will change; 'twas wont to hold me but while one would tell twenty.

First Murderer

How dost thou feel thyself now?

Second Murderer

'Faith, some certain dregs of conscience are yet within me.

First Murderer

Remember our reward, when the deed is done.

Second Murderer

'Zounds, he dies: I had forgot the reward.

First Murderer

Where is thy conscience now?

Second Murderer

In the Duke of Gloucester's purse.

First Murderer

So when he opens his purse to give us our reward, thy conscience flies out.

Second Murderer

Let it go; there's few or none will entertain it.

First Murderer

How if it come to thee again?

Second Murderer

I'll not meddle with it: it is a dangerous thing: it makes a man a coward: a man cannot steal, but it accuseth him; he cannot swear, but it cheques him; he cannot lie with his neighbour's wife, but it detects him: 'tis a blushing shamefast spirit that mutinies in a man's bosom; it fills one full of obstacles: it made me once restore a purse of gold that I found; it beggars any man that keeps it: it is turned out of all towns and cities for a dangerous thing; and every man that means to live well endeavours to trust to himself and to live without it.

First Murderer

'Zounds, it is even now at my elbow, persuading me not to kill the duke.

Second Murderer

Take the devil in thy mind, and relieve him not: he would insinuate with thee but to make thee sigh.

First Murderer

Tut, I am strong-framed, he cannot prevail with me, I warrant thee.

Second Murderer

Spoke like a tail fellow that respects his reputation. Come, shall we to this gear?

First Murderer

Take him over the costard with the hilts of thy sword, and then we will chop him in the malmsey-butt in the next room.

Second Murderer

O excellent devise! make a sop of him.

First Murderer

Hark! he stirs: shall I strike?

Second Murderer

No, first let's reason with him.

CLARENCE

Where art thou, keeper? give me a cup of wine.

Second murderer

You shall have wine enough, my lord, anon.

CLARENCE

In God's name, what art thou?

Second Murderer

A man, as you are.

CLARENCE

But not, as I am, royal.

Second Murderer

Nor you, as we are, loyal.

CLARENCE

Thy voice is thunder, but thy looks are humble.

Second Murderer

My voice is now the king's, my looks mine own.

CLARENCE

How darkly and how deadly dost thou speak!
Your eyes do menace me: why look you pale?
Who sent you hither? Wherefore do you come?

Both

To, to, to--

CLARENCE

To murder me?

Both

Ay, ay.

CLARENCE

You scarcely have the hearts to tell me so,
And therefore cannot have the hearts to do it.
Wherein, my friends, have I offended you?

First Murderer

Offended us you have not, but the king.

CLARENCE

I shall be reconciled to him again.

Second Murderer

Never, my lord; therefore prepare to die.

CLARENCE

Are you call'd forth from out a world of men
To slay the innocent? What is my offence?
Where are the evidence that do accuse me?
What lawful quest have given their verdict up
Unto the frowning judge? or who pronounced
The bitter sentence of poor Clarence' death?
Before I be convict by course of law,
To threaten me with death is most unlawful.
I charge you, as you hope to have redemption
By Christ's dear blood shed for our grievous sins,
That you depart and lay no hands on me
The deed you undertake is damnable.

First Murderer

What we will do, we do upon command.

Second Murderer

And he that hath commanded is the king.

CLARENCE

Erroneous vassal! the great King of kings
Hath in the tables of his law commanded
That thou shalt do no murder: and wilt thou, then,
Spurn at his edict and fulfil a man's?
Take heed; for he holds vengeance in his hands,
To hurl upon their heads that break his law.

Second Murderer

And that same vengeance doth he hurl on thee,
For false forswearing and for murder too:
Thou didst receive the holy sacrament,
To fight in quarrel of the house of Lancaster.

First Murderer

And, like a traitor to the name of God,
Didst break that vow; and with thy treacherous blade
Unrip'dst the bowels of thy sovereign's son.

Second Murderer

Whom thou wert sworn to cherish and defend.

First Murderer

How canst thou urge God's dreadful law to us,
When thou hast broke it in so dear degree?

CLARENCE

Alas! for whose sake did I that ill deed?
For Edward, for my brother, for his sake: Why, sirs,
He sends ye not to murder me for this
For in this sin he is as deep as I.
If God will be revenged for this deed.
O, know you yet, he doth it publicly,
Take not the quarrel from his powerful arm;
He needs no indirect nor lawless course
To cut off those that have offended him.

First Murderer

Who made thee, then, a bloody minister,
When gallant-springing brave Plantagenet,
That princely novice, was struck dead by thee?

CLARENCE

My brother's love, the devil, and my rage.

First Murderer

Thy brother's love, our duty, and thy fault,
Provoke us hither now to slaughter thee.

CLARENCE

Oh, if you love my brother, hate not me;
I am his brother, and I love him well.

If you be hired for meed, go back again,
And I will send you to my brother Gloucester,
Who shall reward you better for my life
Than Edward will for tidings of my death.

Second Murderer

You are deceived, your brother Gloucester hates you.

CLARENCE

O, no, he loves me, and he holds me dear:
Go you to him from me.

Both

Ay, so we will.

CLARENCE

Tell him, when that our princely father York
Bless'd his three sons with his victorious arm,
And charged us from his soul to love each other,
He little thought of this divided friendship:
Bid Gloucester think of this, and he will weep.

First Murderer

Ay, millstones; as be lesson'd us to weep.

CLARENCE

O, do not slander him, for he is kind.

First Murderer

Right,
As snow in harvest. Thou deceivest thyself:
'Tis he that sent us hither now to slaughter thee.

CLARENCE

It cannot be; for when I parted with him,
He hugg'd me in his arms, and swore, with sobs,
That he would labour my delivery.

Second Murderer

Why, so he doth, now he delivers thee
From this world's thraldom to the joys of heaven.

First Murderer

Make peace with God, for you must die, my lord.

CLARENCE

Hast thou that holy feeling in thy soul,
To counsel me to make my peace with God,
And art thou yet to thy own soul so blind,
That thou wilt war with God by murdering me?
Ah, sirs, consider, he that set you on
To do this deed will hate you for the deed.

Second Murderer

What shall we do?

CLARENCE

Relent, and save your souls.

First Murderer

Relent! 'tis cowardly and womanish.

CLARENCE

Not to relent is beastly, savage, devilish.
Which of you, if you were a prince's son,
Being pent from liberty, as I am now,
if two such murderers as yourselves came to you,
Would not entreat for life?
My friend, I spy some pity in thy looks:
O, if thine eye be not a flatterer,
Come thou on my side, and entreat for me,
As you would beg, were you in my distress
A begging prince what beggar pities not?

Second Murderer

Look behind you, my lord.

First Murderer

Take that, and that: if all this will not do,

Stabs him

I'll drown you in the malmsey-butt within.

Exit, with the body

Second Murderer

A bloody deed, and desperately dispatch'd!
How fain, like Pilate, would I wash my hands
Of this most grievous guilty murder done!

Re-enter First Murderer

First Murderer

How now! what mean'st thou, that thou help'st me not?
By heavens, the duke shall know how slack thou art!

Second Murderer

I would he knew that I had saved his brother!
Take thou the fee, and tell him what I say;
For I repent me that the duke is slain.

Exit

First Murderer

So do not I: go, coward as thou art.
Now must I hide his body in some hole,
Until the duke take order for his burial:
And when I have my meed, I must away;
For this will out, and here I must not stay.

ACT II

SCENE I. London. The palace.

Flourish. Enter KING EDWARD IV sick, QUEEN ELIZABETH, DORSET, RIVERS, HASTINGS, BUCKINGHAM, GREY, and others

KING EDWARD IV

Why, so: now have I done a good day's work:
You peers, continue this united league:
I every day expect an embassage
From my Redeemer to redeem me hence;
And now in peace my soul shall part to heaven,
Since I have set my friends at peace on earth.
Rivers and Hastings, take each other's hand;
Dissemble not your hatred, swear your love.

RIVERS

By heaven, my heart is purged from grudging hate:
And with my hand I seal my true heart's love.

HASTINGS

So thrive I, as I truly swear the like!

KING EDWARD IV

Take heed you dally not before your king;
Lest he that is the supreme King of kings
Confound your hidden falsehood, and award
Either of you to be the other's end.

HASTINGS

So prosper I, as I swear perfect love!

RIVERS

And I, as I love Hastings with my heart!

KING EDWARD IV

Madam, yourself are not exempt in this,
Nor your son Dorset, Buckingham, nor you;
You have been factious one against the other,
Wife, love Lord Hastings, let him kiss your hand;
And what you do, do it unfeignedly.

QUEEN ELIZABETH

Here, Hastings; I will never more remember
Our former hatred, so thrive I and mine!

KING EDWARD IV

Dorset, embrace him; Hastings, love lord marquess.

DORSET

This interchange of love, I here protest,
Upon my part shall be unviolable.

HASTINGS

And so swear I, my lord

They embrace

KING EDWARD IV

Now, princely Buckingham, seal thou this league
With thy embracements to my wife's allies,
And make me happy in your unity.

BUCKINGHAM

Whenever Buckingham doth turn his hate
On you or yours,

To the Queen

but with all duteous love
Doth cherish you and yours, God punish me
With hate in those where I expect most love!
When I have most need to employ a friend,
And most assured that he is a friend
Deep, hollow, treacherous, and full of guile,
Be he unto me! this do I beg of God,
When I am cold in zeal to yours.

KING EDWARD IV

A pleasing cordial, princely Buckingham,
is this thy vow unto my sickly heart.
There wanteth now our brother Gloucester here,
To make the perfect period of this peace.

BUCKINGHAM

And, in good time, here comes the noble duke.

Enter GLOUCESTER

GLOUCESTER

Good morrow to my sovereign king and queen:
And, princely peers, a happy time of day!

KING EDWARD IV

Happy, indeed, as we have spent the day.
Brother, we done deeds of charity;
Made peace enmity, fair love of hate,
Between these swelling wrong-incensed peers.

GLOUCESTER

A blessed labour, my most sovereign liege:
Amongst this princely heap, if any here,
By false intelligence, or wrong surmise,
Hold me a foe;
If I unwittingly, or in my rage,
Have aught committed that is hardly borne
By any in this presence, I desire
To reconcile me to his friendly peace:
'Tis death to me to be at enmity;
I hate it, and desire all good men's love.
First, madam, I entreat true peace of you,
Which I will purchase with my duteous service;
Of you, my noble cousin Buckingham,
If ever any grudge were lodged between us;
Of you, Lord Rivers, and, Lord Grey, of you;
That without desert have frown'd on me;
Dukes, earls, lords, gentlemen; indeed, of all.
I do not know that Englishman alive
With whom my soul is any jot at odds

More than the infant that is born to-night
I thank my God for my humility.

QUEEN ELIZABETH

A holy day shall this be kept hereafter:
I would to God all strifes were well compounded.
My sovereign liege, I do beseech your majesty
To take our brother Clarence to your grace.

GLOUCESTER

Why, madam, have I offer'd love for this
To be so bouted in this royal presence?
Who knows not that the noble duke is dead?

They all start

You do him injury to scorn his corse.

RIVERS

Who knows not he is dead! who knows he is?

QUEEN ELIZABETH

All seeing heaven, what a world is this!

BUCKINGHAM

Look I so pale, Lord Dorset, as the rest?

DORSET

Ay, my good lord; and no one in this presence
But his red colour hath forsook his cheeks.

KING EDWARD IV

Is Clarence dead? the order was reversed.

GLOUCESTER

But he, poor soul, by your first order died,
And that a winged Mercury did bear:
Some tardy cripple bore the countermand,
That came too lag to see him buried.
God grant that some, less noble and less loyal,
Nearer in bloody thoughts, but not in blood,
Deserve not worse than wretched Clarence did,
And yet go current from suspicion!

Enter DERBY

DORSET

A boon, my sovereign, for my service done!

KING EDWARD IV

I pray thee, peace: my soul is full of sorrow.

DORSET

I will not rise, unless your highness grant.

KING EDWARD IV

Then speak at once what is it thou demand'st.

DORSET

The forfeit, sovereign, of my servant's life;
Who slew to-day a righteous gentleman
Lately attendant on the Duke of Norfolk.

KING EDWARD IV

Have a tongue to doom my brother's death,
And shall the same give pardon to a slave?
My brother slew no man; his fault was thought,
And yet his punishment was cruel death.
Who sued to me for him? who, in my rage,
Kneel'd at my feet, and bade me be advised
Who spake of brotherhood? who spake of love?
Who told me how the poor soul did forsake
The mighty Warwick, and did fight for me?
Who told me, in the field by Tewksbury
When Oxford had me down, he rescued me,
And said, 'Dear brother, live, and be a king'?
Who told me, when we both lay in the field
Frozen almost to death, how he did lap me
Even in his own garments, and gave himself,
All thin and naked, to the numb cold night?
All this from my remembrance brutish wrath
Sinfully pluck'd, and not a man of you
Had so much grace to put it in my mind.
But when your carters or your waiting-vassals
Have done a drunken slaughter, and defaced
The precious image of our dear Redeemer,
You straight are on your knees for pardon, pardon;

And I unjustly too, must grant it you
But for my brother not a man would speak,
Nor I, ungracious, speak unto myself
For him, poor soul. The proudest of you all
Have been beholding to him in his life;
Yet none of you would once plead for his life.
O God, I fear thy justice will take hold
On me, and you, and mine, and yours for this!
Come, Hastings, help me to my closet.
Oh, poor Clarence!

Exeunt some with KING EDWARD IV and QUEEN MARGARET

GLOUCESTER

This is the fruit of rashness! Mark'd you not
How that the guilty kindred of the queen
Look'd pale when they did hear of Clarence' death?
O, they did urge it still unto the king!
God will revenge it. But come, let us in,
To comfort Edward with our company.

BUCKINGHAM

We wait upon your grace.

Exeunt

SCENE II. The palace.

Enter the DUCHESS OF YORK, with the two children of CLARENCE

Boy

Tell me, good grandam, is our father dead?

DUCHESS OF YORK

No, boy.

Boy

Why do you wring your hands, and beat your breast,
And cry 'O Clarence, my unhappy son!'

Girl

Why do you look on us, and shake your head,
And call us wretches, orphans, castaways
If that our noble father be alive?

DUCHESS OF YORK

My pretty cousins, you mistake me much;
I do lament the sickness of the king.
As loath to lose him, not your father's death;
It were lost sorrow to wail one that's lost.

Boy

Then, grandam, you conclude that he is dead.
The king my uncle is to blame for this:
God will revenge it; whom I will importune
With daily prayers all to that effect.

Girl

And so will I.

DUCHESS OF YORK

Peace, children, peace! the king doth love you well:
Incapable and shallow innocents,
You cannot guess who caused your father's death.

Boy

Grandam, we can; for my good uncle Gloucester
Told me, the king, provoked by the queen,
Devised impeachments to imprison him :
And when my uncle told me so, he wept,
And hugg'd me in his arm, and kindly kiss'd my cheek;
Bade me rely on him as on my father,
And he would love me dearly as his child.

DUCHESS OF YORK

Oh, that deceit should steal such gentle shapes,
And with a virtuous vizard hide foul guile!
He is my son; yea, and therein my shame;
Yet from my dugs he drew not this deceit.

Boy

Think you my uncle did dissemble, grandam?

DUCHESS OF YORK

Ay, boy.

Boy

I cannot think it. Hark! what noise is this?

Enter QUEEN ELIZABETH, with her hair about her ears; RIVERS, and DORSET after her

QUEEN ELIZABETH

Oh, who shall hinder me to wail and weep,
To chide my fortune, and torment myself?
I'll join with black despair against my soul,
And to myself become an enemy.

DUCHESS OF YORK

What means this scene of rude impatience?

QUEEN ELIZABETH

To make an act of tragic violence:
Edward, my lord, your son, our king, is dead.
Why grow the branches now the root is wither'd?
Why wither not the leaves the sap being gone?
If you will live, lament; if die, be brief,
That our swift-winged souls may catch the king's;
Or, like obedient subjects, follow him
To his new kingdom of perpetual rest.

DUCHESS OF YORK

Ah, so much interest have I in thy sorrow
As I had title in thy noble husband!
I have bewept a worthy husband's death,
And lived by looking on his images:
But now two mirrors of his princely semblance
Are crack'd in pieces by malignant death,
And I for comfort have but one false glass,
Which grieves me when I see my shame in him.
Thou art a widow; yet thou art a mother,
And hast the comfort of thy children left thee:
But death hath snatch'd my husband from mine arms,
And pluck'd two crutches from my feeble limbs,
Edward and Clarence. O, what cause have I,
Thine being but a moiety of my grief,
To overgo thy plaints and drown thy cries!

Boy

Good aunt, you wept not for our father's death;
How can we aid you with our kindred tears?

Girl

Our fatherless distress was left unmoan'd;
Your widow-dolour likewise be unwept!

QUEEN ELIZABETH

Give me no help in lamentation;
I am not barren to bring forth complaints
All springs reduce their currents to mine eyes,
That I, being govern'd by the watery moon,
May send forth plenteous tears to drown the world!
Oh for my husband, for my dear lord Edward!

Children

Oh for our father, for our dear lord Clarence!

DUCHESS OF YORK

Alas for both, both mine, Edward and Clarence!

QUEEN ELIZABETH

What stay had I but Edward? and he's gone.

Children

What stay had we but Clarence? and he's gone.

DUCHESS OF YORK

What stays had I but they? and they are gone.

QUEEN ELIZABETH

Was never widow had so dear a loss!

Children

Were never orphans had so dear a loss!

DUCHESS OF YORK

Was never mother had so dear a loss!
Alas, I am the mother of these moans!
Their woes are parcell'd, mine are general.
She for an Edward weeps, and so do I;
I for a Clarence weep, so doth not she:

These babes for Clarence weep and so do I;
I for an Edward weep, so do not they:
Alas, you three, on me, threefold distress'd,
Pour all your tears! I am your sorrow's nurse,
And I will pamper it with lamentations.

DORSET

Comfort, dear mother: God is much displeased
That you take with unthankfulness, his doing:
In common worldly things, 'tis call'd ungrateful,
With dull unwilligness to repay a debt
Which with a bounteous hand was kindly lent;
Much more to be thus opposite with heaven,
For it requires the royal debt it lent you.

RIVERS

Madam, bethink you, like a careful mother,
Of the young prince your son: send straight for him
Let him be crown'd; in him your comfort lives:
Drown desperate sorrow in dead Edward's grave,
And plant your joys in living Edward's throne.

Enter GLOUCESTER, BUCKINGHAM, DERBY, HASTINGS, and RATCLIFF

GLOUCESTER

Madam, have comfort: all of us have cause
To wail the dimming of our shining star;
But none can cure their harms by wailing them.
Madam, my mother, I do cry you mercy;
I did not see your grace: humbly on my knee
I crave your blessing.

DUCHESS OF YORK

God bless thee; and put meekness in thy mind,
Love, charity, obedience, and true duty!

GLOUCESTER

[Aside] Amen; and make me die a good old man!
That is the butt-end of a mother's blessing:
I marvel why her grace did leave it out.

BUCKINGHAM

You cloudy princes and heart-sorrowing peers,
That bear this mutual heavy load of moan,
Now cheer each other in each other's love
Though we have spent our harvest of this king,
We are to reap the harvest of his son.
The broken rancour of your high-swoln hearts,
But lately splinter'd, knit, and join'd together,
Must gently be preserved, cherish'd, and kept:
Me seemeth good, that, with some little train,
Forthwith from Ludlow the young prince be fetch'd
Hither to London, to be crown'd our king.

RIVERS

Why with some little train, my Lord of Buckingham?

BUCKINGHAM

Marry, my lord, lest, by a multitude,
The new-heal'd wound of malice should break out,
Which would be so much the more dangerous
By how much the estate is green and yet ungovern'd:
Where every horse bears his commanding rein,
And may direct his course as please himself,
As well the fear of harm, as harm apparent,
In my opinion, ought to be prevented.

GLOUCESTER

I hope the king made peace with all of us
And the compact is firm and true in me.

RIVERS

And so in me; and so, I think, in all:
Yet, since it is but green, it should be put
To no apparent likelihood of breach,
Which haply by much company might be urged:
Therefore I say with noble Buckingham,
That it is meet so few should fetch the prince.

HASTINGS

And so say I.

GLOUCESTER

Then be it so; and go we to determine
Who they shall be that straight shall post to Ludlow.
Madam, and you, my mother, will you go
To give your censures in this weighty business?

QUEEN ELIZABETH DUCHESS OF YORK

With all our harts.

Exeunt all but BUCKINGHAM and GLOUCESTER

BUCKINGHAM

My lord, whoever journeys to the Prince,
For God's sake, let not us two be behind;
For, by the way, I'll sort occasion,
As index to the story we late talk'd of,
To part the queen's proud kindred from the king.

GLOUCESTER

My other self, my counsel's consistory,
My oracle, my prophet! My dear cousin,
I, like a child, will go by thy direction.
Towards Ludlow then, for we'll not stay behind.

Exeunt

SCENE III. London. A street.

Enter two Citizens meeting

First Citizen

Neighbour, well met: whither away so fast?

Second Citizen

I promise you, I scarcely know myself:
Hear you the news abroad?

First Citizen

Ay, that the king is dead.

Second Citizen

Bad news, by'r lady; seldom comes the better:
I fear, I fear 'twill prove a troublous world.

Enter another Citizen

Third Citizen

Neighbours, God speed!

First Citizen

Give you good morrow, sir.

Third Citizen

Doth this news hold of good King Edward's death?

Second Citizen

Ay, sir, it is too true; God help the while!

Third Citizen

Then, masters, look to see a troublous world.

First Citizen

No, no; by God's good grace his son shall reign.

Third Citizen

Woe to the land that's govern'd by a child!

Second Citizen

In him there is a hope of government,
That in his nonage council under him,
And in his full and ripen'd years himself,
No doubt, shall then and till then govern well.

First Citizen

So stood the state when Henry the Sixth
Was crown'd in Paris but at nine months old.

Third Citizen

Stood the state so? No, no, good friends, God wot;
For then this land was famously enrich'd
With politic grave counsel; then the king
Had virtuous uncles to protect his grace.

First Citizen

Why, so hath this, both by the father and mother.

Third Citizen

Better it were they all came by the father,
Or by the father there were none at all;

For emulation now, who shall be nearest,
Will touch us all too near, if God prevent not.
O, full of danger is the Duke of Gloucester!
And the queen's sons and brothers haught and proud:
And were they to be ruled, and not to rule,
This sickly land might solace as before.

First Citizen

Come, come, we fear the worst; all shall be well.

Third Citizen

When clouds appear, wise men put on their cloaks;
When great leaves fall, the winter is at hand;
When the sun sets, who doth not look for night?
Untimely storms make men expect a dearth.
All may be well; but, if God sort it so,
'Tis more than we deserve, or I expect.

Second Citizen

Truly, the souls of men are full of dread:
Ye cannot reason almost with a man
That looks not heavily and full of fear.

Third Citizen

Before the times of change, still is it so:
By a divine instinct men's minds mistrust
Ensuing dangers; as by proof, we see
The waters swell before a boisterous storm.
But leave it all to God. whither away?

Second Citizen

Marry, we were sent for to the justices.

Third Citizen

And so was I: I'll bear you company.
Exeunt

SCENE IV. London. The palace.

Enter the ARCHBISHOP OF YORK, young YORK, QUEEN ELIZABETH, and the DUCHESS OF YORK

ARCHBISHOP OF YORK

Last night, I hear, they lay at Northampton;
At Stony-Stratford will they be to-night:
To-morrow, or next day, they will be here.

DUCHESS OF YORK

I long with all my heart to see the prince:
I hope he is much grown since last I saw him.

QUEEN ELIZABETH

But I hear, no; they say my son of York
Hath almost overta'en him in his growth.

YORK

Ay, mother; but I would not have it so.

DUCHESS OF YORK

Why, my young cousin, it is good to grow.

YORK

Grandam, one night, as we did sit at supper,
My uncle Rivers talk'd how I did grow
More than my brother: 'Ay,' quoth my uncle Gloucester,
'Small herbs have grace, great weeds do grow apace:'
And since, methinks, I would not grow so fast,
Because sweet flowers are slow and weeds make haste.

DUCHESS OF YORK

Good faith, good faith, the saying did not hold
In him that did object the same to thee;
He was the wretched'st thing when he was young,
So long a-growing and so leisurely,
That, if this rule were true, he should be gracious.

ARCHBISHOP OF YORK

Why, madam, so, no doubt, he is.

DUCHESS OF YORK

I hope he is; but yet let mothers doubt.

YORK

Now, by my troth, if I had been remember'd,
I could have given my uncle's grace a flout,
To touch his growth nearer than he touch'd mine.

DUCHESS OF YORK

How, my pretty York? I pray thee, let me hear it.

YORK

Marry, they say my uncle grew so fast
That he could gnaw a crust at two hours old
'Twas full two years ere I could get a tooth.
Grandam, this would have been a biting jest.

DUCHESS OF YORK

I pray thee, pretty York, who told thee this?

YORK

Grandam, his nurse.

DUCHESS OF YORK

His nurse! why, she was dead ere thou wert born.

YORK

If 'twere not she, I cannot tell who told me.

QUEEN ELIZABETH

A parlous boy: go to, you are too shrewd.

ARCHBISHOP OF YORK

Good madam, be not angry with the child.

QUEEN ELIZABETH

Pitchers have ears.

Enter a Messenger

ARCHBISHOP OF YORK

Here comes a messenger. What news?

Messenger

Such news, my lord, as grieves me to unfold.

QUEEN ELIZABETH

How fares the prince?

Messenger

Well, madam, and in health.

DUCHESS OF YORK

What is thy news then?

Messenger

Lord Rivers and Lord Grey are sent to Pomfret,
With them Sir Thomas Vaughan, prisoners.

DUCHESS OF YORK

Who hath committed them?

Messenger

The mighty dukes
Gloucester and Buckingham.

QUEEN ELIZABETH

For what offence?

Messenger

The sum of all I can, I have disclosed;
Why or for what these nobles were committed
Is all unknown to me, my gracious lady.

QUEEN ELIZABETH

Ay me, I see the downfall of our house!
The tiger now hath seized the gentle hind;
Insulting tyranny begins to jet
Upon the innocent and aweless throne:
Welcome, destruction, death, and massacre!
I see, as in a map, the end of all.

DUCHESS OF YORK

Accursed and unquiet wrangling days,
How many of you have mine eyes beheld!
My husband lost his life to get the crown;
And often up and down my sons were toss'd,
For me to joy and weep their gain and loss:
And being seated, and domestic broils

Clean over-blown, themselves, the conquerors.
Make war upon themselves; blood against blood,
Self against self: O, preposterous
And frantic outrage, end thy damned spleen;
Or let me die, to look on death no more!

QUEEN ELIZABETH

Come, come, my boy; we will to sanctuary.
Madam, farewell.

DUCHESS OF YORK

I'll go along with you.

QUEEN ELIZABETH

You have no cause.

ARCHBISHOP OF YORK

My gracious lady, go;
And thither bear your treasure and your goods.
For my part, I'll resign unto your grace
The seal I keep: and so betide to me
As well I tender you and all of yours!
Come, I'll conduct you to the sanctuary.

Exeunt

ACT III

SCENE I. London. A street.

The trumpets sound. Enter the young PRINCE EDWARD, GLOUCESTER, BUCKINGHAM, CARDINAL, CATESBY, and others

BUCKINGHAM

Welcome, sweet prince, to London, to your chamber.

GLOUCESTER

Welcome, dear cousin, my thoughts' sovereign
The weary way hath made you melancholy.

PRINCE EDWARD

No, uncle; but our crosses on the way
Have made it tedious, wearisome, and heavy
I want more uncles here to welcome me.

GLOUCESTER

Sweet prince, the untainted virtue of your years
Hath not yet dived into the world's deceit
Nor more can you distinguish of a man
Than of his outward show; which, God he knows,
Seldom or never jumpeth with the heart.
Those uncles which you want were dangerous;
Your grace attended to their sugar'd words,
But look'd not on the poison of their hearts :
God keep you from them, and from such false friends!

PRINCE EDWARD

God keep me from false friends! but they were none.

GLOUCESTER

My lord, the mayor of London comes to greet you.

Enter the Lord Mayor and his train

Lord Mayor

God bless your grace with health and happy days!

PRINCE EDWARD

I thank you, good my lord; and thank you all.
I thought my mother, and my brother York,
Would long ere this have met us on the way
Fie, what a slug is Hastings, that he comes not
To tell us whether they will come or no!

Enter HASTINGS

BUCKINGHAM

And, in good time, here comes the sweating lord.

PRINCE EDWARD

Welcome, my lord: what, will our mother come?

HASTINGS

On what occasion, God he knows, not I,
The queen your mother, and your brother York,
Have taken sanctuary: the tender prince
Would fain have come with me to meet your grace,
But by his mother was perforce withheld.

BUCKINGHAM

Fie, what an indirect and peevish course
Is this of hers! Lord cardinal, will your grace
Persuade the queen to send the Duke of York
Unto his princely brother presently?
If she deny, Lord Hastings, go with him,
And from her jealous arms pluck him perforce.

CARDINAL

My Lord of Buckingham, if my weak oratory
Can from his mother win the Duke of York,
Anon expect him here; but if she be obdurate
To mild entreaties, God in heaven forbid

We should infringe the holy privilege
Of blessed sanctuary! not for all this land
Would I be guilty of so deep a sin.

BUCKINGHAM

You are too senseless--obstinate, my lord,
Too ceremonious and traditional
Weigh it but with the grossness of this age,
You break not sanctuary in seizing him.
The benefit thereof is always granted
To those whose dealings have deserved the place,
And those who have the wit to claim the place:
This prince hath neither claim'd it nor deserved it;
And therefore, in mine opinion, cannot have it:
Then, taking him from thence that is not there,
You break no privilege nor charter there.
Oft have I heard of sanctuary men;
But sanctuary children ne'er till now.

CARDINAL

My lord, you shall o'er-rule my mind for once.
Come on, Lord Hastings, will you go with me?

HASTINGS

I go, my lord.

PRINCE EDWARD

Good lords, make all the speedy haste you may.

Exeunt CARDINAL and HASTINGS

Say, uncle Gloucester, if our brother come,
Where shall we sojourn till our coronation?

GLOUCESTER

Where it seems best unto your royal self.
If I may counsel you, some day or two
Your highness shall repose you at the Tower:
Then where you please, and shall be thought most fit
For your best health and recreation.

PRINCE EDWARD

I do not like the Tower, of any place.
Did Julius Caesar build that place, my lord?

BUCKINGHAM

He did, my gracious lord, begin that place;
Which, since, succeeding ages have re-edified.

PRINCE EDWARD

Is it upon record, or else reported
Successively from age to age, he built it?

BUCKINGHAM

Upon record, my gracious lord.

PRINCE EDWARD

But say, my lord, it were not register'd,
Methinks the truth should live from age to age,
As 'twere retail'd to all posterity,
Even to the general all-ending day.

GLOUCESTER

[Aside] So wise so young, they say, do never
live long.

PRINCE EDWARD

What say you, uncle?

GLOUCESTER

I say, without characters, fame lives long.

Aside

Thus, like the formal vice, Iniquity,
I moralize two meanings in one word.

PRINCE EDWARD

That Julius Caesar was a famous man;
With what his valour did enrich his wit,
His wit set down to make his valour live
Death makes no conquest of this conqueror;
For now he lives in fame, though not in life.
I'll tell you what, my cousin Buckingham,--

BUCKINGHAM

What, my gracious lord?

PRINCE EDWARD

An if I live until I be a man,
I'll win our ancient right in France again,
Or die a soldier, as I lived a king.

GLOUCESTER

[Aside] Short summers lightly have a forward spring.

Enter young YORK, HASTINGS, and the CARDINAL

BUCKINGHAM

Now, in good time, here comes the Duke of York.

PRINCE EDWARD

Richard of York! how fares our loving brother?

YORK

Well, my dread lord; so must I call you now.

PRINCE EDWARD

Ay, brother, to our grief, as it is yours:
Too late he died that might have kept that title,
Which by his death hath lost much majesty.

GLOUCESTER

How fares our cousin, noble Lord of York?

YORK

I thank you, gentle uncle. O, my lord,
You said that idle weeds are fast in growth
The prince my brother hath outgrown me far.

GLOUCESTER

He hath, my lord.

YORK

And therefore is he idle?

GLOUCESTER

O, my fair cousin, I must not say so.

YORK

Then is he more beholding to you than I.

GLOUCESTER

He may command me as my sovereign;
But you have power in me as in a kinsman.

YORK

I pray you, uncle, give me this dagger.

GLOUCESTER

My dagger, little cousin? with all my heart.

PRINCE EDWARD

A beggar, brother?

YORK

Of my kind uncle, that I know will give;
And being but a toy, which is no grief to give.

GLOUCESTER

A greater gift than that I'll give my cousin.

YORK

A greater gift! O, that's the sword to it.

GLOUCESTER

A gentle cousin, were it light enough.

YORK

O, then, I see, you will part but with light gifts;
In weightier things you'll say a beggar nay.

GLOUCESTER

It is too heavy for your grace to wear.

YORK

I weigh it lightly, were it heavier.

GLOUCESTER

What, would you have my weapon, little lord?

YORK

I would, that I might thank you as you call me.

GLOUCESTER

How?

YORK

Little.

PRINCE EDWARD

My Lord of York will still be cross in talk:
Uncle, your grace knows how to bear with him.

YORK

You mean, to bear me, not to bear with me:
Uncle, my brother mocks both you and me;
Because that I am little, like an ape,
He thinks that you should bear me on your shoulders.

BUCKINGHAM

With what a sharp-provided wit he reasons!
To mitigate the scorn he gives his uncle,
He prettily and aptly taunts himself:
So cunning and so young is wonderful.

GLOUCESTER

My lord, will't please you pass along?
Myself and my good cousin Buckingham
Will to your mother, to entreat of her
To meet you at the Tower and welcome you.

YORK

What, will you go unto the Tower, my lord?

PRINCE EDWARD

My lord protector needs will have it so.

YORK

I shall not sleep in quiet at the Tower.

GLOUCESTER

Why, what should you fear?

YORK

Marry, my uncle Clarence' angry ghost:
My grandam told me he was murdered there.

PRINCE EDWARD

I fear no uncles dead.

GLOUCESTER

Nor none that live, I hope.

PRINCE EDWARD

An if they live, I hope I need not fear.
But come, my lord; and with a heavy heart,
Thinking on them, go I unto the Tower.

A Sennet. Exeunt all but GLOUCESTER, BUCKINGHAM *and* CATESBY

BUCKINGHAM

Think you, my lord, this little prating York
Was not incensed by his subtle mother
To taunt and scorn you thus opprobriously?

GLOUCESTER

No doubt, no doubt; O, 'tis a parlous boy;
Bold, quick, ingenious, forward, capable
He is all the mother's, from the top to toe.

BUCKINGHAM

Well, let them rest. Come hither, Catesby.
Thou art sworn as deeply to effect what we intend
As closely to conceal what we impart:
Thou know'st our reasons urged upon the way;
What think'st thou? is it not an easy matter
To make William Lord Hastings of our mind,
For the instalment of this noble duke
In the seat royal of this famous isle?

CATESBY

He for his father's sake so loves the prince,
That he will not be won to aught against him.

BUCKINGHAM

What think'st thou, then, of Stanley? what will he?

CATESBY

He will do all in all as Hastings doth.

BUCKINGHAM

Well, then, no more but this: go, gentle Catesby,
And, as it were far off sound thou Lord Hastings,
How doth he stand affected to our purpose;
And summon him to-morrow to the Tower,
To sit about the coronation.
If thou dost find him tractable to us,
Encourage him, and show him all our reasons:
If he be leaden, icy-cold, unwilling,
Be thou so too; and so break off your talk,

And give us notice of his inclination:
For we to-morrow hold divided councils,
Wherein thyself shalt highly be employ'd.

GLOUCESTER

Commend me to Lord William: tell him, Catesby,
His ancient knot of dangerous adversaries
To-morrow are let blood at Pomfret-castle;
And bid my friend, for joy of this good news,
Give mistress Shore one gentle kiss the more.

BUCKINGHAM

Good Catesby, go, effect this business soundly.

CATESBY

My good lords both, with all the heed I may.

GLOUCESTER

Shall we hear from you, Catesby, ere we sleep?

CATESBY

You shall, my lord.

GLOUCESTER

At Crosby Place, there shall you find us both.
Exit CATESBY

BUCKINGHAM

Now, my lord, what shall we do, if we perceive
Lord Hastings will not yield to our complots?

GLOUCESTER

Chop off his head, man; somewhat we will do:
And, look, when I am king, claim thou of me
The earldom of Hereford, and the moveables
Whereof the king my brother stood possess'd.

BUCKINGHAM

I'll claim that promise at your grace's hands.

GLOUCESTER

And look to have it yielded with all willingness.
Come, let us sup betimes, that afterwards
We may digest our complots in some form.
Exeunt

SCENE II. Before Lord Hastings' house.

Enter a Messenger

Messenger
What, ho! my lord!

HASTINGS
[Within] Who knocks at the door?

Messenger
A messenger from the Lord Stanley.

Enter HASTINGS

HASTINGS
What is't o'clock?

Messenger
Upon the stroke of four.

HASTINGS
Cannot thy master sleep these tedious nights?

Messenger
So it should seem by that I have to say.
First, he commends him to your noble lordship.

HASTINGS
And then?

Messenger
And then he sends you word
He dreamt to-night the boar had razed his helm:
Besides, he says there are two councils held;
And that may be determined at the one
which may make you and him to rue at the other.
Therefore he sends to know your lordship's pleasure,
If presently you will take horse with him,
And with all speed post with him toward the north,
To shun the danger that his soul divines.

HASTINGS
Go, fellow, go, return unto thy lord;
Bid him not fear the separated councils
His honour and myself are at the one,
And at the other is my servant Catesby

Where nothing can proceed that toucheth us
Whereof I shall not have intelligence.
Tell him his fears are shallow, wanting instance:
And for his dreams, I wonder he is so fond
To trust the mockery of unquiet slumbers
To fly the boar before the boar pursues,
Were to incense the boar to follow us
And make pursuit where he did mean no chase.
Go, bid thy master rise and come to me
And we will both together to the Tower,
Where, he shall see, the boar will use us kindly.

Messenger

My gracious lord, I'll tell him what you say.

Exit

Enter CATESBY

CATESBY

Many good morrows to my noble lord!

HASTINGS

Good morrow, Catesby; you are early stirring
What news, what news, in this our tottering state?

CATESBY

It is a reeling world, indeed, my lord;
And I believe twill never stand upright
Tim Richard wear the garland of the realm.

HASTINGS

How! wear the garland! dost thou mean the crown?

CATESBY

Ay, my good lord.

HASTINGS

I'll have this crown of mine cut from my shoulders
Ere I will see the crown so foul misplaced.
But canst thou guess that he doth aim at it?

CATESBY

Ay, on my life; and hopes to find forward
Upon his party for the gain thereof:

And thereupon he sends you this good news,
That this same very day your enemies,
The kindred of the queen, must die at Pomfret.

HASTINGS

Indeed, I am no mourner for that news,
Because they have been still mine enemies:
But, that I'll give my voice on Richard's side,
To bar my master's heirs in true descent,
God knows I will not do it, to the death.

CATESBY

God keep your lordship in that gracious mind!

HASTINGS

But I shall laugh at this a twelve-month hence,
That they who brought me in my master's hate
I live to look upon their tragedy.
I tell thee, Catesby--

CATESBY

What, my lord?

HASTINGS

Ere a fortnight make me elder,
I'll send some packing that yet think not on it.

CATESBY

'Tis a vile thing to die, my gracious lord,
When men are unprepared and look not for it.

HASTINGS

O monstrous, monstrous! and so falls it out
With Rivers, Vaughan, Grey: and so 'twill do
With some men else, who think themselves as safe
As thou and I; who, as thou know'st, are dear
To princely Richard and to Buckingham.

CATESBY

The princes both make high account of you;

Aside

For they account his head upon the bridge.

HASTINGS

I know they do; and I have well deserved it.

Enter STANLEY

Come on, come on; where is your boar-spear, man?
Fear you the boar, and go so unprovided?

STANLEY

My lord, good morrow; good morrow, Catesby:
You may jest on, but, by the holy rood,
I do not like these several councils, I.

HASTINGS

My lord,
I hold my life as dear as you do yours;
And never in my life, I do protest,
Was it more precious to me than 'tis now:
Think you, but that I know our state secure,
I would be so triumphant as I am?

STANLEY

The lords at Pomfret, when they rode from London,
Were jocund, and supposed their state was sure,
And they indeed had no cause to mistrust;
But yet, you see how soon the day o'ercast.
This sudden stag of rancour I misdoubt:
Pray God, I say, I prove a needless coward!
What, shall we toward the Tower? the day is spent.

HASTINGS

Come, come, have with you. Wot you what, my lord?
To-day the lords you talk of are beheaded.

LORD STANLEY

They, for their truth, might better wear their heads
Than some that have accused them wear their hats.
But come, my lord, let us away.

Enter a Pursuivant

HASTINGS

Go on before; I'll talk with this good fellow.

Exeunt STANLEY and CATESBY

How now, sirrah! how goes the world with thee?

Pursuivant

The better that your lordship please to ask.

HASTINGS

I tell thee, man, 'tis better with me now
Than when I met thee last where now we meet:
Then was I going prisoner to the Tower,
By the suggestion of the queen's allies;
But now, I tell thee--keep it to thyself--
This day those enemies are put to death,
And I in better state than e'er I was.

Pursuivant

God hold it, to your honour's good content!

HASTINGS

Gramercy, fellow: there, drink that for me.

Throws him his purse

Pursuivant

God save your lordship!

Exit

Enter a Priest

Priest

Well met, my lord; I am glad to see your honour.

HASTINGS

I thank thee, good Sir John, with all my heart.
I am in your debt for your last exercise;
Come the next Sabbath, and I will content you.

He whispers in his ear

Enter BUCKINGHAM

BUCKINGHAM

What, talking with a priest, lord chamberlain?
Your friends at Pomfret, they do need the priest;
Your honour hath no shriving work in hand.

HASTINGS

Good faith, and when I met this holy man,
Those men you talk of came into my mind.
What, go you toward the Tower?

BUCKINGHAM

I do, my lord; but long I shall not stay
I shall return before your lordship thence.

HASTINGS

'Tis like enough, for I stay dinner there.

BUCKINGHAM

[Aside] And supper too, although thou know'st it not.
Come, will you go?

HASTINGS

I'll wait upon your lordship.

Exeunt

SCENE III. Pomfret Castle.

Enter RATCLIFF, with halberds, carrying RIVERS, GREY, and VAUGHAN to death

RATCLIFF

Come, bring forth the prisoners.

RIVERS

Sir Richard Ratcliff, let me tell thee this:
To-day shalt thou behold a subject die
For truth, for duty, and for loyalty.

GREY

God keep the prince from all the pack of you!
A knot you are of damned blood-suckers!

VAUGHAN

You live that shall cry woe for this after.

RATCLIFF

Dispatch; the limit of your lives is out.

RIVERS

O Pomfret, Pomfret! O thou bloody prison,
Fatal and ominous to noble peers!

Within the guilty closure of thy walls
Richard the second here was hack'd to death;
And, for more slander to thy dismal seat,
We give thee up our guiltless blood to drink.

GREY

Now Margaret's curse is fall'n upon our heads,
For standing by when Richard stabb'd her son.

RIVERS

Then cursed she Hastings, then cursed she Buckingham,
Then cursed she Richard. O, remember, God
To hear her prayers for them, as now for us
And for my sister and her princely sons,
Be satisfied, dear God, with our true blood,
Which, as thou know'st, unjustly must be spilt.

RATCLIFF

Make haste; the hour of death is expiate.

RIVERS

Come, Grey, come, Vaughan, let us all embrace:
And take our leave, until we meet in heaven.

Exeunt

SCENE IV. The Tower of London.

Enter BUCKINGHAM, DERBY, HASTINGS, the BISHOP OF ELY, RATCLIFF, LOVEL, with others, and take their seats at a table

HASTINGS

My lords, at once: the cause why we are met
Is, to determine of the coronation.
In God's name, speak: when is the royal day?

BUCKINGHAM

Are all things fitting for that royal time?

DERBY

It is, and wants but nomination.

BISHOP OF ELY

To-morrow, then, I judge a happy day.

BUCKINGHAM

Who knows the lord protector's mind herein?
Who is most inward with the royal duke?

BISHOP OF ELY

Your grace, we think, should soonest know his mind.

BUCKINGHAM

Who, I, my lord I we know each other's faces,
But for our hearts, he knows no more of mine,
Than I of yours;
Nor I no more of his, than you of mine.
Lord Hastings, you and he are near in love.

HASTINGS

I thank his grace, I know he loves me well;
But, for his purpose in the coronation.
I have not sounded him, nor he deliver'd
His gracious pleasure any way therein:
But you, my noble lords, may name the time;
And in the duke's behalf I'll give my voice,
Which, I presume, he'll take in gentle part.
Enter GLOUCESTER

BISHOP OF ELY

Now in good time, here comes the duke himself.

GLOUCESTER

My noble lords and cousins all, good morrow.
I have been long a sleeper; but, I hope,
My absence doth neglect no great designs,
Which by my presence might have been concluded.

BUCKINGHAM

Had not you come upon your cue, my lord
William Lord Hastings had pronounced your part,--
I mean, your voice,--for crowning of the king.

GLOUCESTER

Than my Lord Hastings no man might be bolder;
His lordship knows me well, and loves me well.

HASTINGS

I thank your grace.

GLOUCESTER

My lord of Ely!

BISHOP OF ELY

My lord?

GLOUCESTER

When I was last in Holborn,
I saw good strawberries in your garden there
I do beseech you send for some of them.

BISHOP OF ELY

Marry, and will, my lord, with all my heart.

Exit

GLOUCESTER

Cousin of Buckingham, a word with you.

Drawing him aside

Catesby hath sounded Hastings in our business,
And finds the testy gentleman so hot,
As he will lose his head ere give consent
His master's son, as worshipful as he terms it,
Shall lose the royalty of England's throne.

BUCKINGHAM

Withdraw you hence, my lord, I'll follow you.

Exit GLOUCESTER, BUCKINGHAM following

DERBY

We have not yet set down this day of triumph.
To-morrow, in mine opinion, is too sudden;
For I myself am not so well provided
As else I would be, were the day prolong'd.

Re-enter BISHOP OF ELY

BISHOP OF ELY

Where is my lord protector? I have sent for these strawberries.

HASTINGS

His grace looks cheerfully and smooth to-day;
There's some conceit or other likes him well,
When he doth bid good morrow with such a spirit.
I think there's never a man in Christendom
That can less hide his love or hate than he;
For by his face straight shall you know his heart.

DERBY

What of his heart perceive you in his face
By any likelihood he show'd to-day?

HASTINGS

Marry, that with no man here he is offended;
For, were he, he had shown it in his looks.

DERBY

I pray God he be not, I say.

Re-enter GLOUCESTER and BUCKINGHAM

GLOUCESTER

I pray you all, tell me what they deserve
That do conspire my death with devilish plots
Of damned witchcraft, and that have prevail'd
Upon my body with their hellish charms?

HASTINGS

The tender love I bear your grace, my lord,
Makes me most forward in this noble presence
To doom the offenders, whatsoever they be
I say, my lord, they have deserved death.

GLOUCESTER

Then be your eyes the witness of this ill:
See how I am bewitch'd; behold mine arm
Is, like a blasted sapling, wither'd up:
And this is Edward's wife, that monstrous witch,
Consorted with that harlot strumpet Shore,
That by their witchcraft thus have marked me.

HASTINGS

If they have done this thing, my gracious lord--

GLOUCESTER

If I thou protector of this damned strumpet--
Tellest thou me of 'ifs'? Thou art a traitor:
Off with his head! Now, by Saint Paul I swear,
I will not dine until I see the same.
Lovel and Ratcliff, look that it be done:
The rest, that love me, rise and follow me.

Exeunt all but HASTINGS, RATCLIFF, and LOVEL

HASTINGS

Woe, woe for England! not a whit for me;
For I, too fond, might have prevented this.
Stanley did dream the boar did raze his helm;
But I disdain'd it, and did scorn to fly:
Three times to-day my foot-cloth horse did stumble,
And startled, when he look'd upon the Tower,
As loath to bear me to the slaughter-house.
O, now I want the priest that spake to me:
I now repent I told the pursuivant
As 'twere triumphing at mine enemies,
How they at Pomfret bloodily were butcher'd,
And I myself secure in grace and favour.
O Margaret, Margaret, now thy heavy curse
Is lighted on poor Hastings' wretched head!

RATCLIFF

Dispatch, my lord; the duke would be at dinner:
Make a short shrift; he longs to see your head.

HASTINGS

O momentary grace of mortal men,
Which we more hunt for than the grace of God!
Who builds his hopes in air of your good looks,
Lives like a drunken sailor on a mast,
Ready, with every nod, to tumble down
Into the fatal bowels of the deep.

LOVEL

Come, come, dispatch; 'tis bootless to exclaim.

HASTINGS

O bloody Richard! miserable England!
I prophesy the fearful'st time to thee
That ever wretched age hath look'd upon.
Come, lead me to the block; bear him my head.
They smile at me that shortly shall be dead.
Exeunt

SCENE V. The Tower-walls.

Enter GLOUCESTER and BUCKINGHAM, in rotten armour, marvellous ill-favoured

GLOUCESTER

Come, cousin, canst thou quake, and change thy colour,
Murder thy breath in the middle of a word,
And then begin again, and stop again,
As if thou wert distraught and mad with terror?

BUCKINGHAM

Tut, I can counterfeit the deep tragedian;
Speak and look back, and pry on every side,
Tremble and start at wagging of a straw,
Intending deep suspicion: ghastly looks
Are at my service, like enforced smiles;
And both are ready in their offices,
At any time, to grace my stratagems.
But what, is Catesby gone?

GLOUCESTER

He is; and, see, he brings the mayor along.
Enter the Lord Mayor and CATESBY

BUCKINGHAM

Lord mayor,--

GLOUCESTER

Look to the drawbridge there!

BUCKINGHAM

Hark! a drum.

GLOUCESTER

Catesby, o'erlook the walls.

BUCKINGHAM

Lord mayor, the reason we have sent--

GLOUCESTER

Look back, defend thee, here are enemies.

BUCKINGHAM

God and our innocency defend and guard us!

GLOUCESTER

Be patient, they are friends, Ratcliff and Lovel.
Enter LOVEL and RATCLIFF, with HASTINGS' head

LOVEL

Here is the head of that ignoble traitor,
The dangerous and unsuspected Hastings.

GLOUCESTER

So dear I loved the man, that I must weep.
I took him for the plainest harmless creature
That breathed upon this earth a Christian;
Made him my book wherein my soul recorded
The history of all her secret thoughts:
So smooth he daub'd his vice with show of virtue,
That, his apparent open guilt omitted,
I mean, his conversation with Shore's wife,
He lived from all attainder of suspect.

BUCKINGHAM

Well, well, he was the covert'st shelter'd traitor
That ever lived.
Would you imagine, or almost believe,
Were't not that, by great preservation,
We live to tell it you, the subtle traitor
This day had plotted, in the council-house
To murder me and my good Lord of Gloucester?

Lord Mayor

What, had he so?

GLOUCESTER

What, think You we are Turks or infidels?
Or that we would, against the form of law,
Proceed thus rashly to the villain's death,
But that the extreme peril of the case,
The peace of England and our persons' safety,
Enforced us to this execution?

Lord Mayor

Now, fair befall you! he deserved his death;
And you my good lords, both have well proceeded,
To warn false traitors from the like attempts.
I never look'd for better at his hands,
After he once fell in with Mistress Shore.

GLOUCESTER

Yet had not we determined he should die,
Until your lordship came to see his death;
Which now the loving haste of these our friends,
Somewhat against our meaning, have prevented:
Because, my lord, we would have had you heard
The traitor speak, and timorously confess
The manner and the purpose of his treason;
That you might well have signified the same
Unto the citizens, who haply may
Misconstrue us in him and wail his death.

Lord Mayor

But, my good lord, your grace's word shall serve,
As well as I had seen and heard him speak
And doubt you not, right noble princes both,
But I'll acquaint our duteous citizens
With all your just proceedings in this cause.

GLOUCESTER

And to that end we wish'd your lord-ship here,
To avoid the carping censures of the world.

BUCKINGHAM

But since you come too late of our intents,
Yet witness what you hear we did intend:
And so, my good lord mayor, we bid farewell.

Exit Lord Mayor

GLOUCESTER

Go, after, after, cousin Buckingham.
The mayor towards Guildhall hies him in all post:
There, at your meet'st advantage of the time,
Infer the bastardy of Edward's children:
Tell them how Edward put to death a citizen,
Only for saying he would make his son
Heir to the crown; meaning indeed his house,
Which, by the sign thereof was termed so.
Moreover, urge his hateful luxury
And bestial appetite in change of lust;
Which stretched to their servants, daughters, wives,
Even where his lustful eye or savage heart,
Without control, listed to make his prey.
Nay, for a need, thus far come near my person:
Tell them, when that my mother went with child
Of that unsatiate Edward, noble York
My princely father then had wars in France
And, by just computation of the time,
Found that the issue was not his begot;
Which well appeared in his lineaments,
Being nothing like the noble duke my father:
But touch this sparingly, as 'twere far off,
Because you know, my lord, my mother lives.

BUCKINGHAM

Fear not, my lord, I'll play the orator
As if the golden fee for which I plead
Were for myself: and so, my lord, adieu.

GLOUCESTER

If you thrive well, bring them to Baynard's Castle;
Where you shall find me well accompanied
With reverend fathers and well-learned bishops.

BUCKINGHAM

I go: and towards three or four o'clock
Look for the news that the Guildhall affords.

Exit BUCKINGHAM

GLOUCESTER

Go, Lovel, with all speed to Doctor Shaw;

To CATESBY

Go thou to Friar Penker; bid them both
Meet me within this hour at Baynard's Castle.

Exeunt all but GLOUCESTER

Now will I in, to take some privy order,
To draw the brats of Clarence out of sight;
And to give notice, that no manner of person
At any time have recourse unto the princes.

Exit

SCENE VI. The same.

Enter a Scrivener, with a paper in his hand

Scrivener

This is the indictment of the good Lord Hastings;
Which in a set hand fairly is engross'd,
That it may be this day read over in Paul's.
And mark how well the sequel hangs together:
Eleven hours I spent to write it over,
For yesternight by Catesby was it brought me;
The precedent was full as long a-doing:
And yet within these five hours lived Lord Hastings,
Untainted, unexamined, free, at liberty
Here's a good world the while! Why who's so gross,
That seeth not this palpable device?
Yet who's so blind, but says he sees it not?
Bad is the world; and all will come to nought,
When such bad dealings must be seen in thought.

Exit

SCENE VII. Baynard's Castle.

Enter GLOUCESTER and BUCKINGHAM, at several doors

GLOUCESTER

How now, my lord, what say the citizens?

BUCKINGHAM

Now, by the holy mother of our Lord,
The citizens are mum and speak not a word.

GLOUCESTER

Touch'd you the bastardy of Edward's children?

BUCKINGHAM

I did; with his contract with Lady Lucy,
And his contract by deputy in France;
The insatiate greediness of his desires,
And his enforcement of the city wives;
His tyranny for trifles; his own bastardy,
As being got, your father then in France,
His resemblance, being not like the duke;
Withal I did infer your lineaments,
Being the right idea of your father,
Both in your form and nobleness of mind;
Laid open all your victories in Scotland,
Your dicipline in war, wisdom in peace,
Your bounty, virtue, fair humility:
Indeed, left nothing fitting for the purpose
Untouch'd, or slightly handled, in discourse
And when mine oratory grew to an end
I bid them that did love their country's good
Cry 'God save Richard, England's royal king!'

GLOUCESTER

Ah! and did they so?

BUCKINGHAM

No, so God help me, they spake not a word;
But, like dumb statues or breathing stones,
Gazed each on other, and look'd deadly pale.
Which when I saw, I reprehended them;
And ask'd the mayor what meant this wilful silence:
His answer was, the people were not wont
To be spoke to but by the recorder.
Then he was urged to tell my tale again,
'Thus saith the duke, thus hath the duke inferr'd;'

But nothing spake in warrant from himself.
When he had done, some followers of mine own,
At the lower end of the hall, hurl'd up their caps,
And some ten voices cried 'God save King Richard!'
And thus I took the vantage of those few,
'Thanks, gentle citizens and friends,' quoth I;
'This general applause and loving shout
Argues your wisdoms and your love to Richard:'
And even here brake off, and came away.

GLOUCESTER

What tongueless blocks were they! would not they speak?

BUCKINGHAM

No, by my troth, my lord.

GLOUCESTER

Will not the mayor then and his brethren come?

BUCKINGHAM

The mayor is here at hand: intend some fear;
Be not you spoke with, but by mighty suit:
And look you get a prayer-book in your hand,
And stand betwixt two churchmen, good my lord;
For on that ground I'll build a holy descant:
And be not easily won to our request:
Play the maid's part, still answer nay, and take it.

GLOUCESTER

I go; and if you plead as well for them
As I can say nay to thee for myself,
No doubt well bring it to a happy issue.

BUCKINGHAM

Go, go, up to the leads; the lord mayor knocks.

Exit GLOUCESTER

Enter the Lord Mayor and Citizens

Welcome my lord; I dance attendance here;
I think the duke will not be spoke withal.

Enter CATESBY

Here comes his servant: how now, Catesby,
What says he?

CATESBY

My lord: he doth entreat your grace;
To visit him to-morrow or next day:
He is within, with two right reverend fathers,
Divinely bent to meditation;
And no worldly suit would he be moved,
To draw him from his holy exercise.

BUCKINGHAM

Return, good Catesby, to thy lord again;
Tell him, myself, the mayor and citizens,
In deep designs and matters of great moment,
No less importing than our general good,
Are come to have some conference with his grace.

CATESBY

I'll tell him what you say, my lord.

Exit

BUCKINGHAM

Ah, ha, my lord, this prince is not an Edward!
He is not lolling on a lewd day-bed,
But on his knees at meditation;
Not dallying with a brace of courtezans,
But meditating with two deep divines;
Not sleeping, to engross his idle body,
But praying, to enrich his watchful soul:
Happy were England, would this gracious prince
Take on himself the sovereignty thereof:
But, sure, I fear, we shall ne'er win him to it.

Lord Mayor

Marry, God forbid his grace should say us nay!

BUCKINGHAM

I fear he will.

Re-enter CATESBY

How now, Catesby, what says your lord?

CATESBY

My lord,
He wonders to what end you have assembled
Such troops of citizens to speak with him,
His grace not being warn'd thereof before:
My lord, he fears you mean no good to him.

BUCKINGHAM

Sorry I am my noble cousin should
Suspect me, that I mean no good to him:
By heaven, I come in perfect love to him;
And so once more return and tell his grace.

Exit CATESBY

When holy and devout religious men
Are at their beads, 'tis hard to draw them thence,
So sweet is zealous contemplation.

Enter GLOUCESTER aloft, between two Bishops. CATESBY returns

Lord Mayor

See, where he stands between two clergymen!

BUCKINGHAM

Two props of virtue for a Christian prince,
To stay him from the fall of vanity:
And, see, a book of prayer in his hand,
True ornaments to know a holy man.
Famous Plantagenet, most gracious prince,
Lend favourable ears to our request;
And pardon us the interruption
Of thy devotion and right Christian zeal.

GLOUCESTER

My lord, there needs no such apology:
I rather do beseech you pardon me,
Who, earnest in the service of my God,
Neglect the visitation of my friends.
But, leaving this, what is your grace's pleasure?

BUCKINGHAM

Even that, I hope, which pleaseth God above,
And all good men of this ungovern'd isle.

GLOUCESTER

I do suspect I have done some offence
That seems disgracious in the city's eyes,
And that you come to reprehend my ignorance.

BUCKINGHAM

You have, my lord: would it might please your grace,
At our entreaties, to amend that fault!

GLOUCESTER

Else wherefore breathe I in a Christian land?

BUCKINGHAM

Then know, it is your fault that you resign
The supreme seat, the throne majestical,
The scepter'd office of your ancestors,
Your state of fortune and your due of birth,
The lineal glory of your royal house,
To the corruption of a blemished stock:
Whilst, in the mildness of your sleepy thoughts,
Which here we waken to our country's good,
This noble isle doth want her proper limbs;
Her face defaced with scars of infamy,
Her royal stock graft with ignoble plants,
And almost shoulder'd in the swallowing gulf
Of blind forgetfulness and dark oblivion.
Which to recure, we heartily solicit
Your gracious self to take on you the charge
And kingly government of this your land,
Not as protector, steward, substitute,
Or lowly factor for another's gain;
But as successively from blood to blood,
Your right of birth, your empery, your own.
For this, consorted with the citizens,
Your very worshipful and loving friends,
And by their vehement instigation,
In this just suit come I to move your grace.

GLOUCESTER

I know not whether to depart in silence,
Or bitterly to speak in your reproof.

Best fitteth my degree or your condition
If not to answer, you might haply think
Tongue-tied ambition, not replying, yielded
To bear the golden yoke of sovereignty,
Which fondly you would here impose on me;
If to reprove you for this suit of yours,
So season'd with your faithful love to me.
Then, on the other side, I cheque'd my friends.
Therefore, to speak, and to avoid the first,
And then, in speaking, not to incur the last,
Definitively thus I answer you.
Your love deserves my thanks; but my desert
Unmeritable shuns your high request.
First if all obstacles were cut away,
And that my path were even to the crown,
As my ripe revenue and due by birth
Yet so much is my poverty of spirit,
So mighty and so many my defects,
As I had rather hide me from my greatness,
Being a bark to brook no mighty sea,
Than in my greatness covet to be hid,
And in the vapour of my glory smother'd.
But, God be thank'd, there's no need of me,
And much I need to help you, if need were;
The royal tree hath left us royal fruit,
Which, mellow'd by the stealing hours of time,
Will well become the seat of majesty,
And make, no doubt, us happy by his reign.
On him I lay what you would lay on me,
The right and fortune of his happy stars;
Which God defend that I should wring from him!

BUCKINGHAM

My lord, this argues conscience in your grace;
But the respects thereof are nice and trivial,
All circumstances well considered.
You say that Edward is your brother's son:
So say we too, but not by Edward's wife;
For first he was contract to Lady Lucy--

Your mother lives a witness to that vow--
And afterward by substitute betroth'd
To Bona, sister to the King of France.
These both put by a poor petitioner,
A care-crazed mother of a many children,
A beauty-waning and distressed widow,
Even in the afternoon of her best days,
Made prize and purchase of his lustful eye,
Seduced the pitch and height of all his thoughts
To base declension and loathed bigamy
By her, in his unlawful bed, he got
This Edward, whom our manners term the prince.
More bitterly could I expostulate,
Save that, for reverence to some alive,
I give a sparing limit to my tongue.
Then, good my lord, take to your royal self
This proffer'd benefit of dignity;
If non to bless us and the land withal,
Yet to draw forth your noble ancestry
From the corruption of abusing times,
Unto a lineal true-derived course.

Lord Mayor

Do, good my lord, your citizens entreat you.

BUCKINGHAM

Refuse not, mighty lord, this proffer'd love.

CATESBY

O, make them joyful, grant their lawful suit!

GLOUCESTER

Alas, why would you heap these cares on me?
I am unfit for state and majesty;
I do beseech you, take it not amiss;
I cannot nor I will not yield to you.

BUCKINGHAM

If you refuse it,--as, in love and zeal,
Loath to depose the child, Your brother's son;
As well we know your tenderness of heart

And gentle, kind, effeminate remorse,
Which we have noted in you to your kin,
And egally indeed to all estates,--
Yet whether you accept our suit or no,
Your brother's son shall never reign our king;
But we will plant some other in the throne,
To the disgrace and downfall of your house:
And in this resolution here we leave you.--
Come, citizens: 'zounds! I'll entreat no more.

GLOUCESTER

O, do not swear, my lord of Buckingham.

Exit BUCKINGHAM with the Citizens

CATESBY

Call them again, my lord, and accept their suit.

ANOTHER

Do, good my lord, lest all the land do rue it.

GLOUCESTER

Would you enforce me to a world of care?
Well, call them again. I am not made of stone,
But penetrable to your. kind entreats,
Albeit against my conscience and my soul.

Re-enter BUCKINGHAM and the rest

Cousin of Buckingham, and you sage, grave men,
Since you will buckle fortune on my back,
To bear her burthen, whether I will or no,
I must have patience to endure the load:
But if black scandal or foul-faced reproach
Attend the sequel of your imposition,
Your mere enforcement shall acquittance me
From all the impure blots and stains thereof;
For God he knows, and you may partly see,
How far I am from the desire thereof.

Lord Mayor

God bless your grace! we see it, and will say it.

GLOUCESTER

In saying so, you shall but say the truth.

BUCKINGHAM

Then I salute you with this kingly title:
Long live Richard, England's royal king!

Lord Mayor Citizens

Amen.

BUCKINGHAM

To-morrow will it please you to be crown'd?

GLOUCESTER

Even when you please, since you will have it so.

BUCKINGHAM

To-morrow, then, we will attend your grace:
And so most joyfully we take our leave.

GLOUCESTER

Come, let us to our holy task again.
Farewell, good cousin; farewell, gentle friends.

Exeunt

ACT IV

SCENE I. Before the Tower.

Enter, on one side, QUEEN ELIZABETH, DUCHESS OF YORK, and DORSET; on the other, ANNE, Duchess of Gloucester, leading Lady Margaret Plantagenet, CLARENCE's young Daughter

DUCHESS OF YORK

Who m eets us here? my niece Plantagenet
Led in the hand of her kind aunt of Gloucester?
Now, for my life, she's wandering to the Tower,
On pure heart's love to greet the tender princes.
Daughter, well met.

LADY ANNE

God give your graces both
A happy and a joyful time of day!

QUEEN ELIZABETH

As much to you, good sister! Whither away?

LADY ANNE

No farther than the Tower; and, as I guess,
Upon the like devotion as yourselves,
To gratulate the gentle princes there.

QUEEN ELIZABETH

Kind sister, thanks: we'll enter all together.

Enter BRAKENBURY

And, in good time, here the lieutenant comes.
Master lieutenant, pray you, by your leave,
How doth the prince, and my young son of York?

BRAKENBURY

Right well, dear madam. By your patience,
I may not suffer you to visit them;
The king hath straitly charged the contrary.

QUEEN ELIZABETH

The king! why, who's that?

BRAKENBURY

I cry you mercy: I mean the lord protector.

QUEEN ELIZABETH

The Lord protect him from that kingly title!
Hath he set bounds betwixt their love and me?
I am their mother; who should keep me from them?

DUCHESS OF YORK

I am their fathers mother; I will see them.

LADY ANNE

Their aunt I am in law, in love their mother:
Then bring me to their sights; I'll bear thy blame
And take thy office from thee, on my peril.

BRAKENBURY

No, madam, no; I may not leave it so:
I am bound by oath, and therefore pardon me.

Exit

Enter LORD STANLEY

LORD STANLEY

Let me but meet you, ladies, one hour hence,
And I'll salute your grace of York as mother,
And reverend looker on, of two fair queens.

To LADY ANNE

Come, madam, you must straight to Westminster,
There to be crowned Richard's royal queen.

QUEEN ELIZABETH

O, cut my lace in sunder, that my pent heart
May have some scope to beat, or else I swoon
With this dead-killing news!

LADY ANNE

Despiteful tidings! O unpleasing news!

DORSET

Be of good cheer: mother, how fares your grace?

QUEEN ELIZABETH

O Dorset, speak not to me, get thee hence!
Death and destruction dog thee at the heels;
Thy mother's name is ominous to children.
If thou wilt outstrip death, go cross the seas,
And live with Richmond, from the reach of hell
Go, hie thee, hie thee from this slaughter-house,
Lest thou increase the number of the dead;
And make me die the thrall of Margaret's curse,
Nor mother, wife, nor England's counted queen.

LORD STANLEY

Full of wise care is this your counsel, madam.
Take all the swift advantage of the hours;
You shall have letters from me to my son
To meet you on the way, and welcome you.
Be not ta'en tardy by unwise delay.

DUCHESS OF YORK

O ill-dispersing wind of misery!
O my accursed womb, the bed of death!
A cockatrice hast thou hatch'd to the world,
Whose unavoided eye is murderous.

LORD STANLEY

Come, madam, come; I in all haste was sent.

LADY ANNE

And I in all unwillingness will go.
I would to God that the inclusive verge
Of golden metal that must round my brow
Were red-hot steel, to sear me to the brain!
Anointed let me be with deadly venom,
And die, ere men can say, God save the queen!

QUEEN ELIZABETH

Go, go, poor soul, I envy not thy glory
To feed my humour, wish thyself no harm.

LADY ANNE

No! why? When he that is my husband now
Came to me, as I follow'd Henry's corse,
When scarce the blood was well wash'd from his hands
Which issued from my other angel husband
And that dead saint which then I weeping follow'd;
O, when, I say, I look'd on Richard's face,
This was my wish: 'Be thou,' quoth I, ' accursed,
For making me, so young, so old a widow!
And, when thou wed'st, let sorrow haunt thy bed;
And be thy wife--if any be so mad--
As miserable by the life of thee
As thou hast made me by my dear lord's death!
Lo, ere I can repeat this curse again,
Even in so short a space, my woman's heart
Grossly grew captive to his honey words
And proved the subject of my own soul's curse,
Which ever since hath kept my eyes from rest;
For never yet one hour in his bed
Have I enjoy'd the golden dew of sleep,
But have been waked by his timorous dreams.
Besides, he hates me for my father Warwick;
And will, no doubt, shortly be rid of me.

QUEEN ELIZABETH

Poor heart, adieu! I pity thy complaining.

LADY ANNE

No more than from my soul I mourn for yours.

QUEEN ELIZABETH

Farewell, thou woful welcomer of glory!

LADY ANNE

Adieu, poor soul, that takest thy leave of it!

DUCHESS OF YORK

[To DORSET]
Go thou to Richmond, and good fortune guide thee!

To LADY ANNE

Go thou to Richard, and good angels guard thee!

To QUEEN ELIZABETH

Go thou to sanctuary, and good thoughts possess thee!
I to my grave, where peace and rest lie with me!
Eighty odd years of sorrow have I seen,
And each hour's joy wrecked with a week of teen.

QUEEN ELIZABETH

Stay, yet look back with me unto the Tower.
Pity, you ancient stones, those tender babes
Whom envy hath immured within your walls!
Rough cradle for such little pretty ones!
Rude ragged nurse, old sullen playfellow
For tender princes, use my babies well!
So foolish sorrow bids your stones farewell.

Exeunt

SCENE II. London. The palace.

Sennet. Enter KING RICHARD III, in pomp, crowned; BUCKINGHAM, CATESBY, a page, and others

KING RICHARD III

Stand all apart Cousin of Buckingham!

BUCKINGHAM

My gracious sovereign?

KING RICHARD III

Give me thy hand.

Here he ascendeth his throne

Thus high, by thy advice
And thy assistance, is King Richard seated;
But shall we wear these honours for a day?
Or shall they last, and we rejoice in them?

BUCKINGHAM

Still live they and for ever may they last!

KING RICHARD III

O Buckingham, now do I play the touch,
To try if thou be current gold indeed
Young Edward lives: think now what I would say.

BUCKINGHAM

Say on, my loving lord.

KING RICHARD III

Why, Buckingham, I say, I would be king,

BUCKINGHAM

Why, so you are, my thrice renowned liege.

KING RICHARD III

Ha! am I king? 'tis so: but Edward lives.

BUCKINGHAM

True, noble prince.

KING RICHARD III

O bitter consequence,
That Edward still should live! 'True, noble prince!'
Cousin, thou wert not wont to be so dull:
Shall I be plain? I wish the bastards dead;
And I would have it suddenly perform'd.
What sayest thou? speak suddenly; be brief.

BUCKINGHAM

Your grace may do your pleasure.

KING RICHARD III

Tut, tut, thou art all ice, thy kindness freezeth:
Say, have I thy consent that they shall die?

BUCKINGHAM

Give me some breath, some little pause, my lord
Before I positively herein:
I will resolve your grace immediately.

Exit

CATESBY

[Aside to a stander by]
The king is angry: see, he bites the lip.

KING RICHARD III

I will converse with iron-witted fools
And unrespective boys: none are for me

That look into me with considerate eyes:
High-reaching Buckingham grows circumspect.
Boy!

Page

My lord?

KING RICHARD III

Know'st thou not any whom corrupting gold
Would tempt unto a close exploit of death?

Page

My lord, I know a discontented gentleman,
Whose humble means match not his haughty mind:
Gold were as good as twenty orators,
And will, no doubt, tempt him to any thing.

KING RICHARD III

What is his name?

Page

His name, my lord, is Tyrrel.

KING RICHARD III

I partly know the man: go, call him hither.

Exit Page

The deep-revolving witty Buckingham
No more shall be the neighbour to my counsel:
Hath he so long held out with me untired,
And stops he now for breath?

Enter STANLEY

How now! what news with you?

STANLEY

My lord, I hear the Marquis Dorset's fled
To Richmond, in those parts beyond the sea
Where he abides.

Stands apart

KING RICHARD III

Catesby!

CATESBY

My lord?

KING RICHARD III

Rumour it abroad
That Anne, my wife, is sick and like to die:
I will take order for her keeping close.
Inquire me out some mean-born gentleman,
Whom I will marry straight to Clarence' daughter:
The boy is foolish, and I fear not him.
Look, how thou dream'st! I say again, give out
That Anne my wife is sick and like to die:
About it; for it stands me much upon,
To stop all hopes whose growth may damage me.

Exit CATESBY

I must be married to my brother's daughter,
Or else my kingdom stands on brittle glass.
Murder her brothers, and then marry her!
Uncertain way of gain! But I am in
So far in blood that sin will pluck on sin:
Tear-falling pity dwells not in this eye.

Re-enter Page, with TYRREL

Is thy name Tyrrel?

TYRREL

James Tyrrel, and your most obedient subject.

KING RICHARD III

Art thou, indeed?

TYRREL

Prove me, my gracious sovereign.

KING RICHARD III

Darest thou resolve to kill a friend of mine?

TYRREL

Ay, my lord;
But I had rather kill two enemies.

KING RICHARD III

Why, there thou hast it: two deep enemies,
Foes to my rest and my sweet sleep's disturbers
Are they that I would have thee deal upon:
Tyrrel, I mean those bastards in the Tower.

TYRREL

Let me have open means to come to them,
And soon I'll rid you from the fear of them.

KING RICHARD III

Thou sing'st sweet music. Hark, come hither, Tyrrel
Go, by this token: rise, and lend thine ear:

Whispers

There is no more but so: say it is done,
And I will love thee, and prefer thee too.

TYRREL

'Tis done, my gracious lord.

KING RICHARD III

Shall we hear from thee, Tyrrel, ere we sleep?

TYRREL

Ye shall, my Lord.

Exit

Re-enter BUCKINGHAM

BUCKINGHAM

My Lord, I have consider'd in my mind
The late demand that you did sound me in.

KING RICHARD III

Well, let that pass. Dorset is fled to Richmond.

BUCKINGHAM

I hear that news, my lord.

KING RICHARD III

Stanley, he is your wife's son well, look to it.

BUCKINGHAM

My lord, I claim your gift, my due by promise,
For which your honour and your faith is pawn'd;

The earldom of Hereford and the moveables
The which you promised I should possess.

KING RICHARD III

Stanley, look to your wife; if she convey
Letters to Richmond, you shall answer it.

BUCKINGHAM

What says your highness to my just demand?

KING RICHARD III

As I remember, Henry the Sixth
Did prophesy that Richmond should be king,
When Richmond was a little peevish boy.
A king, perhaps, perhaps,--

BUCKINGHAM

My lord!

KING RICHARD III

How chance the prophet could not at that time
Have told me, I being by, that I should kill him?

BUCKINGHAM

My lord, your promise for the earldom,--

KING RICHARD III

Richmond! When last I was at Exeter,
The mayor in courtesy show'd me the castle,
And call'd it Rougemont: at which name I started,
Because a bard of Ireland told me once
I should not live long after I saw Richmond.

BUCKINGHAM

My Lord!

KING RICHARD III

Ay, what's o'clock?

BUCKINGHAM

I am thus bold to put your grace in mind
Of what you promised me.

KING RICHARD III

Well, but what's o'clock?

BUCKINGHAM

Upon the stroke of ten.

KING RICHARD III

Well, let it strike.

BUCKINGHAM

Why let it strike?

KING RICHARD III

Because that, like a Jack, thou keep'st the stroke
Betwixt thy begging and my meditation.
I am not in the giving vein to-day.

BUCKINGHAM

Why, then resolve me whether you will or no.

KING RICHARD III

Tut, tut,
Thou troublest me; am not in the vein.

Exeunt all but BUCKINGHAM

BUCKINGHAM

Is it even so? rewards he my true service
With such deep contempt made I him king for this?
O, let me think on Hastings, and be gone
To Brecknock, while my fearful head is on!

Exit

SCENE III. The same.

Enter TYRREL

TYRREL

The tyrannous and bloody deed is done.
The most arch of piteous massacre
That ever yet this land was guilty of.
Dighton and Forrest, whom I did suborn
To do this ruthless piece of butchery,

Although they were flesh'd villains, bloody dogs,
Melting with tenderness and kind compassion
Wept like two children in their deaths' sad stories.
'Lo, thus' quoth Dighton, 'lay those tender babes:'
'Thus, thus,' quoth Forrest, 'girdling one another
Within their innocent alabaster arms:
Their lips were four red roses on a stalk,
Which in their summer beauty kiss'd each other.
A book of prayers on their pillow lay;
Which once,' quoth Forrest, 'almost changed my mind;
But O! the devil'--there the villain stopp'd
Whilst Dighton thus told on: 'We smothered
The most replenished sweet work of nature,
That from the prime creation e'er she framed.'
Thus both are gone with conscience and remorse;
They could not speak; and so I left them both,
To bring this tidings to the bloody king.
And here he comes.

Enter KING RICHARD III

All hail, my sovereign liege!

KING RICHARD III

Kind Tyrrel, am I happy in thy news?

TYRREL

If to have done the thing you gave in charge
Beget your happiness, be happy then,
For it is done, my lord.

KING RICHARD III

But didst thou see them dead?

TYRREL

I did, my lord.

KING RICHARD III

And buried, gentle Tyrrel?

TYRREL

The chaplain of the Tower hath buried them;
But how or in what place I do not know.

KING RICHARD III

Come to me, Tyrrel, soon at after supper,
And thou shalt tell the process of their death.
Meantime, but think how I may do thee good,
And be inheritor of thy desire.
Farewell till soon.

Exit TYRREL

The son of Clarence have I pent up close;
His daughter meanly have I match'd in marriage;
The sons of Edward sleep in Abraham's bosom,
And Anne my wife hath bid the world good night.
Now, for I know the Breton Richmond aims
At young Elizabeth, my brother's daughter,
And, by that knot, looks proudly o'er the crown,
To her I go, a jolly thriving wooer.

Enter CATESBY

CATESBY

My lord!

KING RICHARD III

Good news or bad, that thou comest in so bluntly?

CATESBY

Bad news, my lord: Ely is fled to Richmond;
And Buckingham, back'd with the hardy Welshmen,
Is in the field, and still his power increaseth.

KING RICHARD III

Ely with Richmond troubles me more near
Than Buckingham and his rash-levied army.
Come, I have heard that fearful commenting
Is leaden servitor to dull delay;
Delay leads impotent and snail-paced beggary
Then fiery expedition be my wing,
Jove's Mercury, and herald for a king!
Come, muster men: my counsel is my shield;
We must be brief when traitors brave the field.

Exeunt

SCENE IV. Before the palace.

Enter QUEEN MARGARET

QUEEN MARGARET

So, now prosperity begins to mellow
And drop into the rotten mouth of death.
Here in these confines slily have I lurk'd,
To watch the waning of mine adversaries.
A dire induction am I witness to,
And will to France, hoping the consequence
Will prove as bitter, black, and tragical.
Withdraw thee, wretched Margaret: who comes here?

Enter QUEEN ELIZABETH and the DUCHESS OF YORK

QUEEN ELIZABETH

Ah, my young princes! ah, my tender babes!
My unblown flowers, new-appearing sweets!
If yet your gentle souls fly in the air
And be not fix'd in doom perpetual,
Hover about me with your airy wings
And hear your mother's lamentation!

QUEEN MARGARET

Hover about her; say, that right for right
Hath dimm'd your infant morn to aged night.

DUCHESS OF YORK

So many miseries have crazed my voice,
That my woe-wearied tongue is mute and dumb,
Edward Plantagenet, why art thou dead?

QUEEN MARGARET

Plantagenet doth quit Plantagenet.
Edward for Edward pays a dying debt.

QUEEN ELIZABETH

Wilt thou, O God, fly from such gentle lambs,
And throw them in the entrails of the wolf?
When didst thou sleep when such a deed was done?

QUEEN MARGARET

When holy Harry died, and my sweet son.

DUCHESS OF YORK

Blind sight, dead life, poor mortal living ghost,
Woe's scene, world's shame, grave's due by life usurp'd,
Brief abstract and record of tedious days,
Rest thy unrest on England's lawful earth,

Sitting down

Unlawfully made drunk with innocents' blood!

QUEEN ELIZABETH

O, that thou wouldst as well afford a grave
As thou canst yield a melancholy seat!
Then would I hide my bones, not rest them here.
O, who hath any cause to mourn but I?

Sitting down by her

QUEEN MARGARET

If ancient sorrow be most reverend,
Give mine the benefit of seniory,
And let my woes frown on the upper hand.
If sorrow can admit society,

Sitting down with them

Tell o'er your woes again by viewing mine:
I had an Edward, till a Richard kill'd him;
I had a Harry, till a Richard kill'd him:
Thou hadst an Edward, till a Richard kill'd him;
Thou hadst a Richard, till a Richard killed him;

DUCHESS OF YORK

I had a Richard too, and thou didst kill him;
I had a Rutland too, thou holp'st to kill him.

QUEEN MARGARET

Thou hadst a Clarence too, and Richard kill'd him.
From forth the kennel of thy womb hath crept
A hell-hound that doth hunt us all to death:
That dog, that had his teeth before his eyes,
To worry lambs and lap their gentle blood,
That foul defacer of God's handiwork,
That excellent grand tyrant of the earth,

That reigns in galled eyes of weeping souls,
Thy womb let loose, to chase us to our graves.
O upright, just, and true-disposing God,
How do I thank thee, that this carnal cur
Preys on the issue of his mother's body,
And makes her pew-fellow with others' moan!

DUCHESS OF YORK

O Harry's wife, triumph not in my woes!
God witness with me, I have wept for thine.

QUEEN MARGARET

Bear with me; I am hungry for revenge,
And now I cloy me with beholding it.
Thy Edward he is dead, that stabb'd my Edward:
Thy other Edward dead, to quit my Edward;
Young York he is but boot, because both they
Match not the high perfection of my loss:
Thy Clarence he is dead that kill'd my Edward;
And the beholders of this tragic play,
The adulterate Hastings, Rivers, Vaughan, Grey,
Untimely smother'd in their dusky graves.
Richard yet lives, hell's black intelligencer,
Only reserved their factor, to buy souls
And send them thither: but at hand, at hand,
Ensues his piteous and unpitied end:
Earth gapes, hell burns, fiends roar, saints pray.
To have him suddenly convey'd away.
Cancel his bond of life, dear God, I prey,
That I may live to say, The dog is dead!

QUEEN ELIZABETH

O, thou didst prophesy the time would come
That I should wish for thee to help me curse
That bottled spider, that foul bunch-back'd toad!

QUEEN MARGARET

I call'd thee then vain flourish of my fortune;
I call'd thee then poor shadow, painted queen;
The presentation of but what I was;

The flattering index of a direful pageant;
One heaved a-high, to be hurl'd down below;
A mother only mock'd with two sweet babes;
A dream of what thou wert, a breath, a bubble,
A sign of dignity, a garish flag,
To be the aim of every dangerous shot,
A queen in jest, only to fill the scene.
Where is thy husband now? where be thy brothers?
Where are thy children? wherein dost thou, joy?
Who sues to thee and cries 'God save the queen'?
Where be the bending peers that flatter'd thee?
Where be the thronging troops that follow'd thee?
Decline all this, and see what now thou art:
For happy wife, a most distressed widow;
For joyful mother, one that wails the name;
For queen, a very caitiff crown'd with care;
For one being sued to, one that humbly sues;
For one that scorn'd at me, now scorn'd of me;
For one being fear'd of all, now fearing one;
For one commanding all, obey'd of none.
Thus hath the course of justice wheel'd about,
And left thee but a very prey to time;
Having no more but thought of what thou wert,
To torture thee the more, being what thou art.
Thou didst usurp my place, and dost thou not
Usurp the just proportion of my sorrow?
Now thy proud neck bears half my burthen'd yoke;
From which even here I slip my weary neck,
And leave the burthen of it all on thee.
Farewell, York's wife, and queen of sad mischance:
These English woes will make me smile in France.

QUEEN ELIZABETH

O thou well skill'd in curses, stay awhile,
And teach me how to curse mine enemies!

QUEEN MARGARET

Forbear to sleep the nights, and fast the days;
Compare dead happiness with living woe;
Think that thy babes were fairer than they were,

And he that slew them fouler than he is:
Bettering thy loss makes the bad causer worse:
Revolving this will teach thee how to curse.

QUEEN ELIZABETH

My words are dull; O, quicken them with thine!

QUEEN MARGARET

Thy woes will make them sharp, and pierce like mine.

Exit

DUCHESS OF YORK

Why should calamity be full of words?

QUEEN ELIZABETH

Windy attorneys to their client woes,
Airy succeeders of intestate joys,
Poor breathing orators of miseries!
Let them have scope: though what they do impart
Help not all, yet do they ease the heart.

DUCHESS OF YORK

If so, then be not tongue-tied: go with me.
And in the breath of bitter words let's smother
My damned son, which thy two sweet sons smother'd.
I hear his drum: be copious in exclaims.

Enter KING RICHARD III, marching, with drums and trumpets

KING RICHARD III

Who intercepts my expedition?

DUCHESS OF YORK

O, she that might have intercepted thee,
By strangling thee in her accursed womb
From all the slaughters, wretch, that thou hast done!

QUEEN ELIZABETH

Hidest thou that forehead with a golden crown,
Where should be graven, if that right were right,
The slaughter of the prince that owed that crown,
And the dire death of my two sons and brothers?
Tell me, thou villain slave, where are my children?

DUCHESS OF YORK

Thou toad, thou toad, where is thy brother Clarence?
And little Ned Plantagenet, his son?

QUEEN ELIZABETH

Where is kind Hastings, Rivers, Vaughan, Grey?

KING RICHARD III

A flourish, trumpets! strike alarum, drums!
Let not the heavens hear these tell-tale women
Rail on the Lord's enointed: strike, I say!

Flourish. Alarums

Either be patient, and entreat me fair,
Or with the clamorous report of war
Thus will I drown your exclamations.

DUCHESS OF YORK

Art thou my son?

KING RICHARD III

Ay, I thank God, my father, and yourself.

DUCHESS OF YORK

Then patiently hear my impatience.

KING RICHARD III

Madam, I have a touch of your condition,
Which cannot brook the accent of reproof.

DUCHESS OF YORK

O, let me speak!

KING RICHARD III

Do then: but I'll not hear.

DUCHESS OF YORK

I will be mild and gentle in my speech.

KING RICHARD III

And brief, good mother; for I am in haste.

DUCHESS OF YORK

Art thou so hasty? I have stay'd for thee,
God knows, in anguish, pain and agony.

KING RICHARD III

And came I not at last to comfort you?

DUCHESS OF YORK

No, by the holy rood, thou know'st it well,
Thou camest on earth to make the earth my hell.
A grievous burthen was thy birth to me;
Tetchy and wayward was thy infancy;
Thy school-days frightful, desperate, wild, and furious,
Thy prime of manhood daring, bold, and venturous,
Thy age confirm'd, proud, subdued, bloody, treacherous,
More mild, but yet more harmful, kind in hatred:
What comfortable hour canst thou name,
That ever graced me in thy company?

KING RICHARD III

Faith, none, but Humphrey Hour, that call'd your grace
To breakfast once forth of my company.
If I be so disgracious in your sight,
Let me march on, and not offend your grace.
Strike the drum.

DUCHESS OF YORK

I prithee, hear me speak.

KING RICHARD III

You speak too bitterly.

DUCHESS OF YORK

Hear me a word;
For I shall never speak to thee again.

KING RICHARD III

So.

DUCHESS OF YORK

Either thou wilt die, by God's just ordinance,
Ere from this war thou turn a conqueror,
Or I with grief and extreme age shall perish
And never look upon thy face again.

Therefore take with thee my most heavy curse;
Which, in the day of battle, tire thee more
Than all the complete armour that thou wear'st!
My prayers on the adverse party fight;
And there the little souls of Edward's children
Whisper the spirits of thine enemies
And promise them success and victory.
Bloody thou art, bloody will be thy end;
Shame serves thy life and doth thy death attend.
Exit

QUEEN ELIZABETH

Though far more cause, yet much less spirit to curse
Abides in me; I say amen to all.

KING RICHARD III

Stay, madam; I must speak a word with you.

QUEEN ELIZABETH

I have no more sons of the royal blood
For thee to murder: for my daughters, Richard,
They shall be praying nuns, not weeping queens;
And therefore level not to hit their lives.

KING RICHARD III

You have a daughter call'd Elizabeth,
Virtuous and fair, royal and gracious.

QUEEN ELIZABETH

And must she die for this? O, let her live,
And I'll corrupt her manners, stain her beauty;
Slander myself as false to Edward's bed;
Throw over her the veil of infamy:
So she may live unscarr'd of bleeding slaughter,
I will confess she was not Edward's daughter.

KING RICHARD III

Wrong not her birth, she is of royal blood.

QUEEN ELIZABETH

To save her life, I'll say she is not so.

KING RICHARD III

Her life is only safest in her birth.

QUEEN ELIZABETH

And only in that safety died her brothers.

KING RICHARD III

Lo, at their births good stars were opposite.

QUEEN ELIZABETH

No, to their lives bad friends were contrary.

KING RICHARD III

All unavoided is the doom of destiny.

QUEEN ELIZABETH

True, when avoided grace makes destiny:
My babes were destined to a fairer death,
If grace had bless'd thee with a fairer life.

KING RICHARD III

You speak as if that I had slain my cousins.

QUEEN ELIZABETH

Cousins, indeed; and by their uncle cozen'd
Of comfort, kingdom, kindred, freedom, life.
Whose hand soever lanced their tender hearts,
Thy head, all indirectly, gave direction:
No doubt the murderous knife was dull and blunt
Till it was whetted on thy stone-hard heart,
To revel in the entrails of my lambs.
But that still use of grief makes wild grief tame,
My tongue should to thy ears not name my boys
Till that my nails were anchor'd in thine eyes;
And I, in such a desperate bay of death,
Like a poor bark, of sails and tackling reft,
Rush all to pieces on thy rocky bosom.

KING RICHARD III

Madam, so thrive I in my enterprise
And dangerous success of bloody wars,

As I intend more good to you and yours,
Than ever you or yours were by me wrong'd!

QUEEN ELIZABETH

What good is cover'd with the face of heaven,
To be discover'd, that can do me good?

KING RICHARD III

The advancement of your children, gentle lady.

QUEEN ELIZABETH

Up to some scaffold, there to lose their heads?

KING RICHARD III

No, to the dignity and height of honour
The high imperial type of this earth's glory.

QUEEN ELIZABETH

Flatter my sorrows with report of it;
Tell me what state, what dignity, what honour,
Canst thou demise to any child of mine?

KING RICHARD III

Even all I have; yea, and myself and all,
Will I withal endow a child of thine;
So in the Lethe of thy angry soul
Thou drown the sad remembrance of those wrongs
Which thou supposest I have done to thee.

QUEEN ELIZABETH

Be brief, lest that be process of thy kindness
Last longer telling than thy kindness' date.

KING RICHARD III

Then know, that from my soul I love thy daughter.

QUEEN ELIZABETH

My daughter's mother thinks it with her soul.

KING RICHARD III

What do you think?

QUEEN ELIZABETH

That thou dost love my daughter from thy soul:
So from thy soul's love didst thou love her brothers;
And from my heart's love I do thank thee for it.

KING RICHARD III

Be not so hasty to confound my meaning:
I mean, that with my soul I love thy daughter,
And mean to make her queen of England.

QUEEN ELIZABETH

Say then, who dost thou mean shall be her king?

KING RICHARD III

Even he that makes her queen who should be else?

QUEEN ELIZABETH

What, thou?

KING RICHARD III

I, even I: what think you of it, madam?

QUEEN ELIZABETH

How canst thou woo her?

KING RICHARD III

That would I learn of you,
As one that are best acquainted with her humour.

QUEEN ELIZABETH

And wilt thou learn of me?

KING RICHARD III

Madam, with all my heart.

QUEEN ELIZABETH

Send to her, by the man that slew her brothers,
A pair of bleeding-hearts; thereon engrave
Edward and York; then haply she will weep:
Therefore present to her--as sometime Margaret
Did to thy father, steep'd in Rutland's blood,--
A handkerchief; which, say to her, did drain
The purple sap from her sweet brother's body
And bid her dry her weeping eyes therewith.
If this inducement force her not to love,
Send her a story of thy noble acts;
Tell her thou madest away her uncle Clarence,

Her uncle Rivers; yea, and, for her sake,
Madest quick conveyance with her good aunt Anne.

KING RICHARD III

Come, come, you mock me; this is not the way
To win our daughter.

QUEEN ELIZABETH

There is no other way
Unless thou couldst put on some other shape,
And not be Richard that hath done all this.

KING RICHARD III

Say that I did all this for love of her.

QUEEN ELIZABETH

Nay, then indeed she cannot choose but hate thee,
Having bought love with such a bloody spoil.

KING RICHARD III

Look, what is done cannot be now amended:
Men shall deal unadvisedly sometimes,
Which after hours give leisure to repent.
If I did take the kingdom from your sons,
To make amends, Ill give it to your daughter.
If I have kill'd the issue of your womb,
To quicken your increase, I will beget
Mine issue of your blood upon your daughter
A grandam's name is little less in love
Than is the doting title of a mother;
They are as children but one step below,
Even of your mettle, of your very blood;
Of an one pain, save for a night of groans
Endured of her, for whom you bid like sorrow.
Your children were vexation to your youth,
But mine shall be a comfort to your age.
The loss you have is but a son being king,
And by that loss your daughter is made queen.
I cannot make you what amends I would,
Therefore accept such kindness as I can.
Dorset your son, that with a fearful soul

Leads discontented steps in foreign soil,
This fair alliance quickly shall call home
To high promotions and great dignity:
The king, that calls your beauteous daughter wife.
Familiarly shall call thy Dorset brother;
Again shall you be mother to a king,
And all the ruins of distressful times
Repair'd with double riches of content.
What! we have many goodly days to see:
The liquid drops of tears that you have shed
Shall come again, transform'd to orient pearl,
Advantaging their loan with interest
Of ten times double gain of happiness.
Go, then my mother, to thy daughter go
Make bold her bashful years with your experience;
Prepare her ears to hear a wooer's tale
Put in her tender heart the aspiring flame
Of golden sovereignty; acquaint the princess
With the sweet silent hours of marriage joys
And when this arm of mine hath chastised
The petty rebel, dull-brain'd Buckingham,
Bound with triumphant garlands will I come
And lead thy daughter to a conqueror's bed;
To whom I will retail my conquest won,
And she shall be sole victress, Caesar's Caesar.

QUEEN ELIZABETH

What were I best to say? her father's brother
Would be her lord? or shall I say, her uncle?
Or, he that slew her brothers and her uncles?
Under what title shall I woo for thee,
That God, the law, my honour and her love,
Can make seem pleasing to her tender years?

KING RICHARD III

Infer fair England's peace by this alliance.

QUEEN ELIZABETH

Which she shall purchase with still lasting war.

KING RICHARD III
Say that the king, which may command, entreats.
QUEEN ELIZABETH
That at her hands which the king's King forbids.
KING RICHARD III
Say, she shall be a high and mighty queen.
QUEEN ELIZABETH
To wail the tide, as her mother doth.
KING RICHARD III
Say, I will love her everlastingly.
QUEEN ELIZABETH
But how long shall that title 'ever' last?
KING RICHARD III
Sweetly in force unto her fair life's end.
QUEEN ELIZABETH
But how long fairly shall her sweet lie last?
KING RICHARD III
So long as heaven and nature lengthens it.
QUEEN ELIZABETH
So long as hell and Richard likes of it.
KING RICHARD III
Say, I, her sovereign, am her subject love.
QUEEN ELIZABETH
But she, your subject, loathes such sovereignty.
KING RICHARD III
Be eloquent in my behalf to her.
QUEEN ELIZABETH
An honest tale speeds best being plainly told.
KING RICHARD III
Then in plain terms tell her my loving tale.
QUEEN ELIZABETH
Plain and not honest is too harsh a style.
KING RICHARD III
Your reasons are too shallow and too quick.

QUEEN ELIZABETH
O no, my reasons are too deep and dead;
Too deep and dead, poor infants, in their grave.
KING RICHARD III
Harp not on that string, madam; that is past.
QUEEN ELIZABETH
Harp on it still shall I till heart-strings break.
KING RICHARD III
Now, by my George, my garter, and my crown,--
QUEEN ELIZABETH
Profaned, dishonour'd, and the third usurp'd.
KING RICHARD III
I swear--
QUEEN ELIZABETH
By nothing; for this is no oath:
The George, profaned, hath lost his holy honour;
The garter, blemish'd, pawn'd his knightly virtue;
The crown, usurp'd, disgraced his kingly glory.
if something thou wilt swear to be believed,
Swear then by something that thou hast not wrong'd.
KING RICHARD III
Now, by the world--
QUEEN ELIZABETH
'Tis full of thy foul wrongs.
KING RICHARD III
My father's death--
QUEEN ELIZABETH
Thy life hath that dishonour'd.
KING RICHARD III
Then, by myself--
QUEEN ELIZABETH
Thyself thyself misusest.
KING RICHARD III
Why then, by God--

QUEEN ELIZABETH
God's wrong is most of all.
If thou hadst fear'd to break an oath by Him,
The unity the king thy brother made
Had not been broken, nor my brother slain:
If thou hadst fear'd to break an oath by Him,
The imperial metal, circling now thy brow,
Had graced the tender temples of my child,
And both the princes had been breathing here,
Which now, two tender playfellows to dust,
Thy broken faith hath made a prey for worms.
What canst thou swear by now?

KING RICHARD III
The time to come.

QUEEN ELIZABETH
That thou hast wronged in the time o'erpast;
For I myself have many tears to wash
Hereafter time, for time past wrong'd by thee.
The children live, whose parents thou hast slaughter'd,
Ungovern'd youth, to wail it in their age;
The parents live, whose children thou hast butcher'd,
Old wither'd plants, to wail it with their age.
Swear not by time to come; for that thou hast
Misused ere used, by time misused o'erpast.

KING RICHARD III
As I intend to prosper and repent,
So thrive I in my dangerous attempt
Of hostile arms! myself myself confound!
Heaven and fortune bar me happy hours!
Day, yield me not thy light; nor, night, thy rest!
Be opposite all planets of good luck
To my proceedings, if, with pure heart's love,
Immaculate devotion, holy thoughts,
I tender not thy beauteous princely daughter!
In her consists my happiness and thine;
Without her, follows to this land and me,

To thee, herself, and many a Christian soul,
Death, desolation, ruin and decay:
It cannot be avoided but by this;
It will not be avoided but by this.
Therefore, good mother,--I must can you so--
Be the attorney of my love to her:
Plead what I will be, not what I have been;
Not my deserts, but what I will deserve:
Urge the necessity and state of times,
And be not peevish-fond in great designs.

QUEEN ELIZABETH

Shall I be tempted of the devil thus?

KING RICHARD III

Ay, if the devil tempt thee to do good.

QUEEN ELIZABETH

Shall I forget myself to be myself?

KING RICHARD III

Ay, if yourself's remembrance wrong yourself.

QUEEN ELIZABETH

But thou didst kill my children.

KING RICHARD III

But in your daughter's womb I bury them:
Where in that nest of spicery they shall breed
Selves of themselves, to your recomforture.

QUEEN ELIZABETH

Shall I go win my daughter to thy will?

KING RICHARD III

And be a happy mother by the deed.

QUEEN ELIZABETH

I go. Write to me very shortly.
And you shall understand from me her mind.

KING RICHARD III

Bear her my true love's kiss; and so, farewell.

Exit QUEEN ELIZABETH

Relenting fool, and shallow, changing woman!

Enter RATCLIFF; CATESBY following

How now! what news?

RATCLIFF

My gracious sovereign, on the western coast
Rideth a puissant navy; to the shore
Throng many doubtful hollow-hearted friends,
Unarm'd, and unresolved to beat them back:
'Tis thought that Richmond is their admiral;
And there they hull, expecting but the aid
Of Buckingham to welcome them ashore.

KING RICHARD III

Some light-foot friend post to the Duke of Norfolk:
Ratcliff, thyself, or Catesby; where is he?

CATESBY

Here, my lord.

KING RICHARD III

Fly to the duke:

To RATCLIFF

Post thou to Salisbury
When thou comest thither--

To CATESBY

Dull, unmindful villain,
Why stand'st thou still, and go'st not to the duke?

CATESBY

First, mighty sovereign, let me know your mind,
What from your grace I shall deliver to him.

KING RICHARD III

O, true, good Catesby: bid him levy straight
The greatest strength and power he can make,
And meet me presently at Salisbury.

CATESBY

I go.

Exit

RATCLIFF

What is't your highness' pleasure I shall do at
Salisbury?

KING RICHARD III

Why, what wouldst thou do there before I go?

RATCLIFF

Your highness told me I should post before.

KING RICHARD III

My mind is changed, sir, my mind is changed.

Enter STANLEY

How now, what news with you?

STANLEY

None good, my lord, to please you with the hearing;
Nor none so bad, but it may well be told.

KING RICHARD III

Hoyday, a riddle! neither good nor bad!
Why dost thou run so many mile about,
When thou mayst tell thy tale a nearer way?
Once more, what news?

STANLEY

Richmond is on the seas.

KING RICHARD III

There let him sink, and be the seas on him!
White-liver'd runagate, what doth he there?

STANLEY

I know not, mighty sovereign, but by guess.

KING RICHARD III

Well, sir, as you guess, as you guess?

STANLEY

Stirr'd up by Dorset, Buckingham, and Ely,
He makes for England, there to claim the crown.

KING RICHARD III

Is the chair empty? is the sword unsway'd?
Is the king dead? the empire unpossess'd?
What heir of York is there alive but we?
And who is England's king but great York's heir?
Then, tell me, what doth he upon the sea?

STANLEY

Unless for that, my liege, I cannot guess.

KING RICHARD III

Unless for that he comes to be your liege,
You cannot guess wherefore the Welshman comes.
Thou wilt revolt, and fly to him, I fear.

STANLEY

No, mighty liege; therefore mistrust me not.

KING RICHARD III

Where is thy power, then, to beat him back?
Where are thy tenants and thy followers?
Are they not now upon the western shore.
Safe-conducting the rebels from their ships!

STANLEY

No, my good lord, my friends are in the north.

KING RICHARD III

Cold friends to Richard: what do they in the north,
When they should serve their sovereign in the west?

STANLEY

They have not been commanded, mighty sovereign:
Please it your majesty to give me leave,
I'll muster up my friends, and meet your grace
Where and what time your majesty shall please.

KING RICHARD III

Ay, ay. thou wouldst be gone to join with Richmond:
I will not trust you, sir.

STANLEY

Most mighty sovereign,
You have no cause to hold my friendship doubtful:
I never was nor never will be false.

KING RICHARD III
Well,
Go muster men; but, hear you, leave behind
Your son, George Stanley: look your faith be firm.
Or else his head's assurance is but frail.

STANLEY
So deal with him as I prove true to you.

Exit

Enter a Messenger

Messenger
My gracious sovereign, now in Devonshire,
As I by friends am well advertised,
Sir Edward Courtney, and the haughty prelate
Bishop of Exeter, his brother there,
With many more confederates, are in arms.

Enter another Messenger

Second Messenger
My liege, in Kent the Guildfords are in arms;
And every hour more competitors
Flock to their aid, and still their power increaseth.

Enter another Messenger

Third Messenger
My lord, the army of the Duke of Buckingham--

KING RICHARD III
Out on you, owls! nothing but songs of death?

He striketh him

Take that, until thou bring me better news.

Third Messenger
The news I have to tell your majesty
Is, that by sudden floods and fall of waters,
Buckingham's army is dispersed and scatter'd;
And he himself wander'd away alone,
No man knows whither.

KING RICHARD III

I cry thee mercy:
There is my purse to cure that blow of thine.
Hath any well-advised friend proclaim'd
Reward to him that brings the traitor in?

Third Messenger

Such proclamation hath been made, my liege.

Enter another Messenger

Fourth Messenger

Sir Thomas Lovel and Lord Marquis Dorset,
'Tis said, my liege, in Yorkshire are in arms.
Yet this good comfort bring I to your grace,
The Breton navy is dispersed by tempest:
Richmond, in Yorkshire, sent out a boat
Unto the shore, to ask those on the banks
If they were his assistants, yea or no;
Who answer'd him, they came from Buckingham.
Upon his party: he, mistrusting them,
Hoisted sail and made away for Brittany.

KING RICHARD III

March on, march on, since we are up in arms;
If not to fight with foreign enemies,
Yet to beat down these rebels here at home.

Re-enter CATESBY

CATESBY

My liege, the Duke of Buckingham is taken;
That is the best news: that the Earl of Richmond
Is with a mighty power landed at Milford,
Is colder tidings, yet they must be told.

KING RICHARD III

Away towards Salisbury! while we reason here,
A royal battle might be won and lost
Some one take order Buckingham be brought
To Salisbury; the rest march on with me.

Flourish. Exeunt

SCENE V. Lord Derby's house.

Enter DERBY and SIR CHRISTOPHER URSWICK

DERBY

Sir Christopher, tell Richmond this from me:
That in the sty of this most bloody boar
My son George Stanley is frank'd up in hold:
If I revolt, off goes young George's head;
The fear of that withholds my present aid.
But, tell me, where is princely Richmond now?

CHRISTOPHER

At Pembroke, or at Harford-west, in Wales.

DERBY

What men of name resort to him?

CHRISTOPHER

Sir Walter Herbert, a renowned soldier;
Sir Gilbert Talbot, Sir William Stanley;
Oxford, redoubted Pembroke, Sir James Blunt,
And Rice ap Thomas with a valiant crew;
And many more of noble fame and worth:
And towards London they do bend their course,
If by the way they be not fought withal.

DERBY

Return unto thy lord; commend me to him:
Tell him the queen hath heartily consented
He shall espouse Elizabeth her daughter.
These letters will resolve him of my mind. Farewell.

Exeunt

ACT V

SCENE I. Salisbury.
An open place.

Enter the Sheriff, and BUCKINGHAM, with halberds, led to execution

BUCKINGHAM

Will not King Richard let me speak with him?

Sheriff

No, my good lord; therefore be patient.

BUCKINGHAM

Hastings, and Edward's children, Rivers, Grey,
Holy King Henry, and thy fair son Edward,
Vaughan, and all that have miscarried
By underhand corrupted foul injustice,
If that your moody discontented souls
Do through the clouds behold this present hour,
Even for revenge mock my destruction!
This is All-Souls' day, fellows, is it not?

Sheriff

It is, my lord.

BUCKINGHAM

Why, then All-Souls' day is my body's doomsday.
This is the day that, in King Edward's time,
I wish't might fall on me, when I was found

False to his children or his wife's allies
This is the day wherein I wish'd to fall
By the false faith of him I trusted most;
This, this All-Souls' day to my fearful soul
Is the determined respite of my wrongs:
That high All-Seer that I dallied with
Hath turn'd my feigned prayer on my head
And given in earnest what I begg'd in jest.
Thus doth he force the swords of wicked men
To turn their own points on their masters' bosoms:
Now Margaret's curse is fallen upon my head;
'When he,' quoth she, 'shall split thy heart with sorrow,
Remember Margaret was a prophetess.'
Come, sirs, convey me to the block of shame;
Wrong hath but wrong, and blame the due of blame.
Exeunt

SCENE II. The camp near Tamworth.

Enter RICHMOND, OXFORD, BLUNT, HERBERT, and others, with drum and colours

RICHMOND

Fellows in arms, and my most loving friends,
Bruised underneath the yoke of tyranny,
Thus far into the bowels of the land
Have we march'd on without impediment;
And here receive we from our father Stanley
Lines of fair comfort and encouragement.
The wretched, bloody, and usurping boar,
That spoil'd your summer fields and fruitful vines,
Swills your warm blood like wash, and makes his trough
In your embowell'd bosoms, this foul swine
Lies now even in the centre of this isle,
Near to the town of Leicester, as we learn
From Tamworth thither is but one day's march.
In God's name, cheerly on, courageous friends,

To reap the harvest of perpetual peace
By this one bloody trial of sharp war.

OXFORD

Every man's conscience is a thousand swords,
To fight against that bloody homicide.

HERBERT

I doubt not but his friends will fly to us.

BLUNT

He hath no friends but who are friends for fear.
Which in his greatest need will shrink from him.

RICHMOND

All for our vantage. Then, in God's name, march:
True hope is swift, and flies with swallow's wings:
Kings it makes gods, and meaner creatures kings.

Exeunt

SCENE III. Bosworth Field.

Enter KING RICHARD III in arms, with NORFOLK, SURREY, and others

KING RICHARD III

Here pitch our tents, even here in Bosworth field.
My Lord of Surrey, why look you so sad?

SURREY

My heart is ten times lighter than my looks.

KING RICHARD III

My Lord of Norfolk,--

NORFOLK

Here, most gracious liege.

KING RICHARD III

Norfolk, we must have knocks; ha! must we not?

NORFOLK

We must both give and take, my gracious lord.

KING RICHARD III

Up with my tent there! here will I lie tonight;
But where to-morrow? Well, all's one for that.
Who hath descried the number of the foe?

NORFOLK

Six or seven thousand is their utmost power.

KING RICHARD III

Why, our battalion trebles that account:
Besides, the king's name is a tower of strength,
Which they upon the adverse party want.
Up with my tent there! Valiant gentlemen,
Let us survey the vantage of the field
Call for some men of sound direction
Let's want no discipline, make no delay,
For, lords, to-morrow is a busy day.

Exeunt

Enter, on the other side of the field, RICHMOND, Sir William Brandon, OXFORD, and others. Some of the Soldiers pitch RICHMOND's tent

RICHMOND

The weary sun hath made a golden set,
And by the bright track of his fiery car,
Gives signal, of a goodly day to-morrow.
Sir William Brandon, you shall bear my standard.
Give me some ink and paper in my tent
I'll draw the form and model of our battle,
Limit each leader to his several charge,
And part in just proportion our small strength.
My Lord of Oxford, you, Sir William Brandon,
And you, Sir Walter Herbert, stay with me.

The Earl of Pembroke keeps his regiment:
Good Captain Blunt, bear my good night to him
And by the second hour in the morning
Desire the earl to see me in my tent:
Yet one thing more, good Blunt, before thou go'st,
Where is Lord Stanley quarter'd, dost thou know?

BLUNT

Unless I have mista'en his colours much,
Which well I am assured I have not done,
His regiment lies half a mile at least
South from the mighty power of the king.

RICHMOND

If without peril it be possible,
Good Captain Blunt, bear my good-night to him,
And give him from me this most needful scroll.

BLUNT

Upon my life, my lord, I'll under-take it;
And so, God give you quiet rest to-night!

RICHMOND

Good night, good Captain Blunt. Come gentlemen,
Let us consult upon to-morrow's business
In to our tent; the air is raw and cold.

They withdraw into the tent

Enter, to his tent, KING RICHARD III, NORFOLK, RATCLIFF, CATESBY, and others

KING RICHARD III

What is't o'clock?

CATESBY

It's supper-time, my lord;
It's nine o'clock.

KING RICHARD III

I will not sup to-night.
Give me some ink and paper.
What, is my beaver easier than it was?
And all my armour laid into my tent?

CATESBY

If is, my liege; and all things are in readiness.

KING RICHARD III

Good Norfolk, hie thee to thy charge;
Use careful watch, choose trusty sentinels.

NORFOLK

I go, my lord.

KING RICHARD III

Stir with the lark to-morrow, gentle Norfolk.

NORFOLK

I warrant you, my lord.

Exit

KING RICHARD III

Catesby!

CATESBY

My lord?

KING RICHARD III

Send out a pursuivant at arms
To Stanley's regiment; bid him bring his power
Before sunrising, lest his son George fall
Into the blind cave of eternal night.

Exit CATESBY

Fill me a bowl of wine. Give me a watch.
Saddle white Surrey for the field to-morrow.
Look that my staves be sound, and not too heavy.
Ratcliff!

RATCLIFF

My lord?

KING RICHARD III

Saw'st thou the melancholy Lord Northumberland?

RATCLIFF

Thomas the Earl of Surrey, and himself,
Much about cock-shut time, from troop to troop
Went through the army, cheering up the soldiers.

KING RICHARD III

So, I am satisfied. Give me a bowl of wine:
I have not that alacrity of spirit,
Nor cheer of mind, that I was wont to have.
Set it down. Is ink and paper ready?

RATCLIFF

It is, my lord.

KING RICHARD III

Bid my guard watch; leave me.
Ratcliff, about the mid of night come to my tent
And help to arm me. Leave me, I say.

Exeunt RATCLIFF and the other Attendants

Enter DERBY to RICHMOND in his tent, Lords and others attending

DERBY

Fortune and victory sit on thy helm!

RICHMOND

All comfort that the dark night can afford
Be to thy person, noble father-in-law!
Tell me, how fares our loving mother?

DERBY

I, by attorney, bless thee from thy mother
Who prays continually for Richmond's good:

So much for that. The silent hours steal on,
And flaky darkness breaks within the east.
In brief,--for so the season bids us be,--
Prepare thy battle early in the morning,
And put thy fortune to the arbitrement
Of bloody strokes and mortal-staring war.
I, as I may--that which I would I cannot,--
With best advantage will deceive the time,
And aid thee in this doubtful shock of arms:
But on thy side I may not be too forward
Lest, being seen, thy brother, tender George,
Be executed in his father's sight.
Farewell: the leisure and the fearful time
Cuts off the ceremonious vows of love
And ample interchange of sweet discourse,
Which so long sunder'd friends should dwell upon:
God give us leisure for these rites of love!
Once more, adieu: be valiant, and speed well!

RICHMOND

Good lords, conduct him to his regiment:
I'll strive, with troubled thoughts, to take a nap,
Lest leaden slumber peise me down to-morrow,
When I should mount with wings of victory:
Once more, good night, kind lords and gentlemen.

Exeunt all but RICHMOND

O Thou, whose captain I account myself,
Look on my forces with a gracious eye;
Put in their hands thy bruising irons of wrath,
That they may crush down with a heavy fall
The usurping helmets of our adversaries!
Make us thy ministers of chastisement,
That we may praise thee in the victory!
To thee I do commend my watchful soul,
Ere I let fall the windows of mine eyes:
Sleeping and waking, O, defend me still!

Sleeps

Enter the Ghost of Prince Edward, son to King Henry VI

Ghost

of Prince Edward

[To KING RICHARD III]
Let me sit heavy on thy soul to-morrow!
Think, how thou stab'dst me in my prime of youth
At Tewksbury: despair, therefore, and die!

To RICHMOND

Be cheerful, Richmond; for the wronged souls
Of butcher'd princes fight in thy behalf
King Henry's issue, Richmond, comforts thee.

Enter the Ghost of King Henry VI

Ghost

of King Henry VI

[To KING RICHARD III]
When I was mortal, my anointed body
By thee was punched full of deadly holes
Think on the Tower and me: despair, and die!
Harry the Sixth bids thee despair, and die!

To RICHMOND

Virtuous and holy, be thou conqueror!
Harry, that prophesied thou shouldst be king,
Doth comfort thee in thy sleep: live, and flourish!

Enter the Ghost of CLARENCE

Ghost of CLARENCE

[To KING RICHARD III]
Let me sit heavy on thy soul to-morrow!
I, that was wash'd to death with fulsome wine,
Poor Clarence, by thy guile betrayed to death!
To-morrow in the battle think on me,
And fall thy edgeless sword: despair, and die!--

To RICHMOND

Thou offspring of the house of Lancaster
The wronged heirs of York do pray for thee
Good angels guard thy battle! live, and flourish!

Enter the Ghosts of RIVERS, GRAY, and VAUGHAN

Ghost of RIVERS

[To KING RICHARD III]
Let me sit heavy on thy soul to-morrow,
Rivers. that died at Pomfret! despair, and die!

Ghost of GREY

[To KING RICHARD III]
Think upon Grey, and let thy soul despair!

Ghost of VAUGHAN

[To KING RICHARD III]
Think upon Vaughan, and, with guilty fear,
Let fall thy lance: despair, and die!

All

[To RICHMOND]
Awake, and think our wrongs in Richard's bosom
Will conquer him! awake, and win the day!

Enter the Ghost of HASTINGS

Ghost of HASTINGS

[To KING RICHARD III]
Bloody and guilty, guiltily awake,
And in a bloody battle end thy days!
Think on Lord Hastings: despair, and die!

To RICHMOND

Quiet untroubled soul, awake, awake!
Arm, fight, and conquer, for fair England's sake!

Enter the Ghosts of the two young Princes

Ghosts

of young Princes

[To KING RICHARD III]
Dream on thy cousins smother'd in the Tower:
Let us be led within thy bosom, Richard,
And weigh thee down to ruin, shame, and death!
Thy nephews' souls bid thee despair and die!

To RICHMOND

Sleep, Richmond, sleep in peace, and wake in joy;
Good angels guard thee from the boar's annoy!
Live, and beget a happy race of kings!
Edward's unhappy sons do bid thee flourish.

Enter the Ghost of LADY ANNE

Ghost of LADY ANNE

[To KING RICHARD III]
Richard, thy wife, that wretched Anne thy wife,
That never slept a quiet hour with thee,
Now fills thy sleep with perturbations
To-morrow in the battle think on me,
And fall thy edgeless sword: despair, and die!

To RICHMOND

Thou quiet soul, sleep thou a quiet sleep
Dream of success and happy victory!
Thy adversary's wife doth pray for thee.

Enter the Ghost of BUCKINGHAM

Ghost

of BUCKINGHAM

[To KING RICHARD III]
The last was I that helped thee to the crown;
The last was I that felt thy tyranny:
O, in the battle think on Buckingham,
And die in terror of thy guiltiness!

Dream on, dream on, of bloody deeds and death:
Fainting, despair; despairing, yield thy breath!

To RICHMOND

I died for hope ere I could lend thee aid:
But cheer thy heart, and be thou not dismay'd:
God and good angel fight on Richmond's side;
And Richard falls in height of all his pride.

The Ghosts vanish

KING RICHARD III starts out of his dream

KING RICHARD III

Give me another horse: bind up my wounds.
Have mercy, Jesu!--Soft! I did but dream.
O coward conscience, how dost thou afflict me!
The lights burn blue. It is now dead midnight.
Cold fearful drops stand on my trembling flesh.
What do I fear? myself? there's none else by:
Richard loves Richard; that is, I am I.
Is there a murderer here? No. Yes, I am:
Then fly. What, from myself? Great reason why:
Lest I revenge. What, myself upon myself?
Alack. I love myself. Wherefore? for any good
That I myself have done unto myself?
O, no! alas, I rather hate myself
For hateful deeds committed by myself!
I am a villain: yet I lie. I am not.
Fool, of thyself speak well: fool, do not flatter.
My conscience hath a thousand several tongues,
And every tongue brings in a several tale,
And every tale condemns me for a villain.
Perjury, perjury, in the high'st degree
Murder, stem murder, in the direst degree;
All several sins, all used in each degree,
Throng to the bar, crying all, Guilty! guilty!
I shall despair. There is no creature loves me;

And if I die, no soul shall pity me:
Nay, wherefore should they, since that I myself
Find in myself no pity to myself?
Methought the souls of all that I had murder'd
Came to my tent; and every one did threat
To-morrow's vengeance on the head of Richard.

Enter RATCLIFF

RATCLIFF

My lord!

KING RICHARD III

'Zounds! who is there?

RATCLIFF

Ratcliff, my lord; 'tis I. The early village-cock
Hath twice done salutation to the morn;
Your friends are up, and buckle on their armour.

KING RICHARD III

O Ratcliff, I have dream'd a fearful dream!
What thinkest thou, will our friends prove all true?

RATCLIFF

No doubt, my lord.

KING RICHARD III

O Ratcliff, I fear, I fear,--

RATCLIFF

Nay, good my lord, be not afraid of shadows.

KING RICHARD III

By the apostle Paul, shadows to-night
Have struck more terror to the soul of Richard
Than can the substance of ten thousand soldiers
Armed in proof, and led by shallow Richmond.
It is not yet near day. Come, go with me;

Under our tents I'll play the eaves-dropper,
To see if any mean to shrink from me.

Exeunt

Enter the Lords to RICHMOND, sitting in his tent

LORDS

Good morrow, Richmond!

RICHMOND

Cry mercy, lords and watchful gentlemen,
That you have ta'en a tardy sluggard here.

LORDS

How have you slept, my lord?

RICHMOND

The sweetest sleep, and fairest-boding dreams
That ever enter'd in a drowsy head,
Have I since your departure had, my lords.
Methought their souls, whose bodies Richard murder'd,
Came to my tent, and cried on victory:
I promise you, my soul is very jocund
In the remembrance of so fair a dream.
How far into the morning is it, lords?

LORDS

Upon the stroke of four.

RICHMOND

Why, then 'tis time to arm and give direction.

His oration to his soldiers

More than I have said, loving countrymen,
The leisure and enforcement of the time
Forbids to dwell upon: yet remember this,
God and our good cause fight upon our side;
The prayers of holy saints and wronged souls,
Like high-rear'd bulwarks, stand before our faces;

Richard except, those whom we fight against
Had rather have us win than him they follow:
For what is he they follow? truly, gentlemen,
A bloody tyrant and a homicide;
One raised in blood, and one in blood establish'd;
One that made means to come by what he hath,
And slaughter'd those that were the means to help him;
Abase foul stone, made precious by the foil
Of England's chair, where he is falsely set;
One that hath ever been God's enemy:
Then, if you fight against God's enemy,
God will in justice ward you as his soldiers;
If you do sweat to put a tyrant down,
You sleep in peace, the tyrant being slain;
If you do fight against your country's foes,
Your country's fat shall pay your pains the hire;
If you do fight in safeguard of your wives,
Your wives shall welcome home the conquerors;
If you do free your children from the sword,
Your children's children quit it in your age.
Then, in the name of God and all these rights,
Advance your standards, draw your willing swords.
For me, the ransom of my bold attempt
Shall be this cold corpse on the earth's cold face;
But if I thrive, the gain of my attempt
The least of you shall share his part thereof.
Sound drums and trumpets boldly and cheerfully;
God and Saint George! Richmond and victory!

Exeunt

Re-enter KING RICHARD, RATCLIFF, Attendants and Forces

KING RICHARD III

What said Northumberland as touching Richmond?

RATCLIFF

That he was never trained up in arms.

KING RICHARD III

He said the truth: and what said Surrey then?

RATCLIFF

He smiled and said 'The better for our purpose.'

KING RICHARD III

He was in the right; and so indeed it is.

Clock striketh

Ten the clock there. Give me a calendar.
Who saw the sun to-day?

RATCLIFF

Not I, my lord.

KING RICHARD III

Then he disdains to shine; for by the book
He should have braved the east an hour ago
A black day will it be to somebody. Ratcliff!

RATCLIFF

My lord?

KING RICHARD III

The sun will not be seen to-day;
The sky doth frown and lour upon our army.
I would these dewy tears were from the ground.
Not shine to-day! Why, what is that to me
More than to Richmond? for the selfsame heaven
That frowns on me looks sadly upon him.

Enter NORFOLK

NORFOLK

Arm, arm, my lord; the foe vaunts in the field.

KING RICHARD III

Come, bustle, bustle; caparison my horse.
Call up Lord Stanley, bid him bring his power:

I will lead forth my soldiers to the plain,
And thus my battle shall be ordered:
My foreward shall be drawn out all in length,
Consisting equally of horse and foot;
Our archers shall be placed in the midst
John Duke of Norfolk, Thomas Earl of Surrey,
Shall have the leading of this foot and horse.
They thus directed, we will follow
In the main battle, whose puissance on either side
Shall be well winged with our chiefest horse.
This, and Saint George to boot! What think'st thou, Norfolk?

NORFOLK

A good direction, warlike sovereign.
This found I on my tent this morning.

He sheweth him a paper

KING RICHARD III

[Reads]
'Jockey of Norfolk, be not too bold,
For Dickon thy master is bought and sold.'
A thing devised by the enemy.
Go, gentleman, every man unto his charge
Let not our babbling dreams affright our souls:
Conscience is but a word that cowards use,
Devised at first to keep the strong in awe:
Our strong arms be our conscience, swords our law.
March on, join bravely, let us to't pell-mell
If not to heaven, then hand in hand to hell.

His oration to his Army

What shall I say more than I have inferr'd?
Remember whom you are to cope withal;
A sort of vagabonds, rascals, and runaways,
A scum of Bretons, and base lackey peasants,
Whom their o'er-cloyed country vomits forth
To desperate ventures and assured destruction.

You sleeping safe, they bring to you unrest;
You having lands, and blest with beauteous wives,
They would restrain the one, distain the other.
And who doth lead them but a paltry fellow,
Long kept in Bretagne at our mother's cost?
A milk-sop, one that never in his life
Felt so much cold as over shoes in snow?
Let's whip these stragglers o'er the seas again;
Lash hence these overweening rags of France,
These famish'd beggars, weary of their lives;
Who, but for dreaming on this fond exploit,
For want of means, poor rats, had hang'd themselves:
If we be conquer'd, let men conquer us,
And not these bastard Bretons; whom our fathers
Have in their own land beaten, bobb'd, and thump'd,
And in record, left them the heirs of shame.
Shall these enjoy our lands? lie with our wives?
Ravish our daughters?

Drum afar off

Hark! I hear their drum.
Fight, gentlemen of England! fight, bold yoemen!
Draw, archers, draw your arrows to the head!
Spur your proud horses hard, and ride in blood;
Amaze the welkin with your broken staves!

Enter a Messenger

What says Lord Stanley? will he bring his power?

Messenger

My lord, he doth deny to come.

KING RICHARD III

Off with his son George's head!

NORFOLK

My lord, the enemy is past the marsh
After the battle let George Stanley die.

KING RICHARD III

A thousand hearts are great within my bosom:
Advance our standards, set upon our foes
Our ancient word of courage, fair Saint George,
Inspire us with the spleen of fiery dragons!
Upon them! victory sits on our helms.

Exeunt

SCENE IV. Another part of the field.

Alarum: excursions. Enter NORFOLK and forces fighting; to him CATESBY

CATESBY

Rescue, my Lord of Norfolk, rescue, rescue!
The king enacts more wonders than a man,
Daring an opposite to every danger:
His horse is slain, and all on foot he fights,
Seeking for Richmond in the throat of death.
Rescue, fair lord, or else the day is lost!

Alarums. Enter KING RICHARD III

KING RICHARD III

A horse! a horse! my kingdom for a horse!

CATESBY

Withdraw, my lord; I'll help you to a horse.

KING RICHARD III

Slave, I have set my life upon a cast,
And I will stand the hazard of the die:
I think there be six Richmonds in the field;
Five have I slain to-day instead of him.
A horse! a horse! my kingdom for a horse!

Exeunt

SCENE V. Another part of the field.

Alarum. Enter KING RICHARD III and RICHMOND; they fight. KING RICHARD III is slain. Retreat and flourish. Re-enter RICHMOND, DERBY bearing the crown, with divers other Lords

RICHMOND

God and your arms be praised, victorious friends,
The day is ours, the bloody dog is dead.

DERBY

Courageous Richmond, well hast thou acquit thee.
Lo, here, this long-usurped royalty
From the dead temples of this bloody wretch
Have I pluck'd off, to grace thy brows withal:
Wear it, enjoy it, and make much of it.

RICHMOND

Great God of heaven, say Amen to all!
But, tell me, is young George Stanley living?

DERBY

He is, my lord, and safe in Leicester town;
Whither, if it please you, we may now withdraw us.

RICHMOND

What men of name are slain on either side?

DERBY

John Duke of Norfolk, Walter Lord Ferrers,
Sir Robert Brakenbury, and Sir William Brandon.

RICHMOND

Inter their bodies as becomes their births:
Proclaim a pardon to the soldiers fled
That in submission will return to us:
And then, as we have ta'en the sacrament,
We will unite the white rose and the red:
Smile heaven upon this fair conjunction,

That long have frown'd upon their enmity!
What traitor hears me, and says not amen?
England hath long been mad, and scarr'd herself;
The brother blindly shed the brother's blood,
The father rashly slaughter'd his own son,
The son, compell'd, been butcher to the sire:
All this divided York and Lancaster,
Divided in their dire division,
O, now, let Richmond and Elizabeth,
The true succeeders of each royal house,
By God's fair ordinance conjoin together!
And let their heirs, God, if thy will be so.
Enrich the time to come with smooth-faced peace,
With smiling plenty and fair prosperous days!
Abate the edge of traitors, gracious Lord,
That would reduce these bloody days again,
And make poor England weep in streams of blood!
Let them not live to taste this land's increase
That would with treason wound this fair land's peace!
Now civil wounds are stopp'd, peace lives again:
That she may long live here, God say amen!
Exeunt